MY GERMAN QUESTION

Books by Peter Gay

The Bourgeois Experience: Victoria to Freud
(5 vols., 1984–1998)

Reading Freud: Explorations and Entertainments (Yale, 1990)

Freud: A Life for Our Time (1988)

A Godless Jew:
Freud, Atheism, and the Making of Psychoanalysis (Yale, 1987)

Freud for Historians (1985)

Freud, Jews, and Other Germans:
Masters and Victims in Modernist Culture (1978)

Art and Act: On Causes in History–Manet, Groupius, Mondrian (1976)

Style in History (1974)

Modern Europe (1973), with R. K. Webb

The Bridge of Criticism: Dialogues on the
Enlightenment (1970)

The Enlightenment: An Interpretation (2 vols., 1966–1969)

Weimar Culture: The Outsider as Insider (1968)

A Loss of Mastery: Puritan Historians in Colonial America (1966)

The Party of Humanity:
Essays in the French Enlightenment (1964)

Voltaire's Politics: The Poet as Realist (1959; rpt. Yale, 1988)

The Dilemma of Democratic Socialism:
Eduard Bernstein's Challenge to Marx (1952)

My German Question

Growing Up in Nazi Berlin

PETER GAY

YALE UNIVERSITY PRESS

NEW HAVEN & LONDON

Designed by James J. Johnson and set in Fairfield Medium type by Rainsford
Type, Danbury, Connecticut.
Printed in the United States of America by R. R. Donnelley, Harrisonburg,
Virginia.

Library of Congress Cataloging-in-Publication Data

Gay, Peter, 1923–
    My German question : growing up in Nazi Berlin / Peter Gay.
        p.   cm.
    ISBN 0-300-07670-3 (alk. paper)

    1. Gay, Peter, 1923–   —Childhood and youth.   2. Jews—Germany—
Berlin.   3. National socialism—Germany—Berlin.   4. Jews—Germany—
History—1933–1945.   5. Jews—Persecutions—Germany—Berlin.
I. Title
DS135.G5G39   1998
943'.155004924'0092—dc21   98-26686

A catalogue record for this book is available from the British Library.

The paper in this book meets the guidelines for permanence and durability of
the Committee on Production Guidelines for Book Longevity of the Council
on Library Resources.

10   9   8   7   6   5   4   3   2

To Emil Busse

Why, this is hell, nor am I out of it.

CHRISTOPHER MARLOWE, *Dr. Faustus*

Contents

Preface

This is not an autobiography; it is a memoir that focuses on the six years, 1933 to 1939, I spent as a boy in Nazi Berlin. Because I have aimed at more than a superficial recital of the outrages I witnessed and the insults I swallowed, I have surrounded my principal plot with chapters in which I diagnose just what I brought to that experience and what deposits it left on me. This book records one man's story, the story of a poisoning and how I dealt with it. But after listening to scores of refugees across the years, I am confident that what I have to say has more general application.

I have not been silent about my past. In two brief essays, I rehearsed some memorable episodes in my life that will reappear in this account. But here both the narrative scale and my analytical intentions are far more ambitious than those of its slight predecessors. The book's origins go back to an informal talk I gave about a dozen years ago to a group of fellows and undergraduates at Yale's Davenport College on the invitation of my friend and colleague Henry Turner, then master of that college. The audience was gratifying in size and attentiveness alike, and my presentation generated an intense discussion and the kind of autobiographical anecdotes that are a regular feature on such occasions. Afterward, it occurred to Henry and me that we should have recorded the evening. My determination to make good this lapse, only reinforced by persuasive friends, is the ultimate source of this book. When Gladys Topkis, one of the most durable among these friends and a fine editor, invited me to write it, this long-cherished plan became a realistic enterprise.

For reasons I did not initially appreciate, this has proved a far harder, far more disturbing assignment than I had expected. The intimates who cheered me on virtually promised me that writing my memoir would afford me a long-needed catharsis, that the exploration of my early years would bring me peace of mind. But the promise was not fulfilled. My emotions remain mixed, and ease of mind plays at best a subordinate role. I have derived considerable satisfaction from putting on the record my contempt for those who, with condescension and 20-20 hindsight, have berated the German Jews for attempting to blend into German society and for not emigrating sooner. I felt gratitude to those who saved us in the desperate times of 1938 and 1939—and rage, surprisingly fierce after all these years, rage at the world for having been so callous to our plight. My hatred for Nazis past and present did not grow with the passage of time, only because it could hardly do so without my committing mayhem on the next German I encountered. No catharsis here!

This, I have said, is not an autobiography, a disclaimer I want to underscore. For this memoir of enduring a hell in the making necessarily has a melancholy tone that, taken by itself, distorts my personal history. The minor mode, which dominates this book, represents only part of me. That there has been a large measure of suffering in my past is a truth I cannot conscientiously deny, and there are times, I fear, when I have made others suffer in consequence. But as I read over this account, I find that in small matters and large, I have accentuated the negative at the expense of the positive. My chosen theme, of course, made this emphasis inescapable. If I wanted to be faithful to what I had proposed to do, I had to set aside much of the savor of the life I have enjoyed.

Take my appetite for music, which appears here mainly in an anecdote about Nazi mendacity and a comment on my parents' puzzlement at my favorite recordings. As a teenager in Havana, I discovered Bing Crosby and the Andrews Sisters. (I am not defending my choices, I am only reporting them.) Once in the United States, I graduated to Glenn Miller and Artie Shaw, and then to Beethoven's quartets. I owe this leap to Harvey Potthoff, my friend for more than half a century, who in the year that I met him, 1943, played for me the last of these masterpieces, opus 135. Another old friend, Bob Webb, cured me of my snobbish conviction that Brahms is an unworthy candidate for the affection of serious music lovers. Similarly, beyond noting that I developed a fleeting infatuation with the fiction of Ernest Hemingway shortly after my arrival in the United States in 1941, this book is silent about my pleasures in the classics of modernist literature, Proust and Joyce and Henry James, some of whose writings I first learned to value through—in fact, whose very existence I first discovered in—Malcolm Cowley's columns in *The New Republic*, essays that were to me, a fledgling and uninformed American, an invaluable resource.

I have been just as reticent about my professional career. I would be driving modesty to the point of absurdity if I minimized or denied my successes. There is nothing here about my teaching or my publications—or what there is serves only to put a spotlight on those terrible years I spent in Hitler's Germany. Yet obviously enough these accomplishments have loomed large in the segments of my life in which the Third Reich played no part. I have been almost as reserved about one of the greatest blessings I have been fortunate enough to enjoy: friendship. I still miss Richard Hofstadter and Henry Roberts, both of whom died untimely in 1970, and I wish they could have read this account of a past about which I talked to them freely. And, to put it tersely, I have been lucky in love. Almost none of these ingredients have found their way into this memoir.

Why, then, undertake it? The question has particular point in a decade when confessions, the more uninhibited the better, have become a best-selling genre. But I thought I should risk it, even though I do not write about celebrities, list honorary degrees or medals, or dwell on sexual abuse—except for a failed attempt. I was bound to agree that my experience included some dramatic episodes worthy of being captured in print. And then there was my academic disposition to didacticism. I had heard, more often than I liked, disparagement of German Jews in the United States, usually laced with self-righteous anger. The decisive confrontation came about four years ago in Berlin, where I had an eye-opening discussion with an influential, intelligent, and decent German public servant with whom I spoke openly about current politics and ancient (which is to say: Nazi) history. One day, looking worried and puzzled, he confessed his failure to understand why Germany's Jews in Hitler's Reich had gone to their slaughter like lambs (he actually used this cliché). His admission inadvertently demonstrated to me more powerfully than ever that even the well-informed were ignorant about the life of Jews under the Nazis. Most seemed content to rehash facile legends, unaware that the truth was much more complicated.

And so I asked myself, Why didn't we pack our bags and leave the country the day after Hitler came to power? It was an agonizing question that I am going to ask again and again in these pages. I came to believe that I could appear as a witness for the defense as well as taking satisfaction from unsparing self-examination—and, I hope, giving satisfaction as well. Whether I have succeeded is not for me to say. But if I thought I had failed I would not have published this book.

MY GERMAN QUESTION

Return of the Native

On June 27, 1961, we crossed the Rhine Bridge from Strasbourg to Kehl, and I was subjected to the most disconcerting anti-Semitic display I had endured since I left Germany twenty-two years earlier. After a delightful few weeks touring in France, my wife, Ruth, and I were on our way to Berlin. A colleague in Columbia's German department, Henry Hatfield, was giving a course on Thomas Mann at the Free University in West Berlin and had invited us to hear him lecture. Touring through France had been an unmitigated delight. We moved westward at a stately pace through the château country all the way to Angers, with its magnificent tapestries, eating and drinking our way across the region. Then we turned south to take in cities like Bordeaux, getting slightly drunk at a dégustation at Château d'Yquem on the sweet local dessert wine, sleeping in double beds guarded by crucifixes overhead. In contrast, our prospects for a German stay seemed far from inviting.

The Free University, its very name a calculated provocation to its East Berlin ancestor, was an institution born or, rather, assembled faculty by faculty, department by department, not long after the war. From 1948 on, academics from the old University of Berlin began to set up new headquarters in idyllic Dahlem. (The old university was renamed Humboldt University by East Germany's Stalinist masters to exploit the great prestige enjoyed by Wilhelm von Humboldt, the humanist who more than anyone had been responsible for the founding of the university in 1810—and who, no doubt, would have been among the first to be arrested in the communist regime.) Dahlem, a district of broad avenues and once magnificent villas, had been spared the worst of Allied bombings, but like all of Berlin it showed the blemishes left by the war. Its avenues were still largely intact, but the villas had been turned into discreet boarding houses and small hotels. This had been a Berlin out of my family's reach, but its famous Grunewald, a sizable, carefully cultivated forest, was familiar to me: as a boy, I had ridden my bicycle in its designated paths.

The academic experiment in Dahlem was a symptom of the deep clefts that polarized the shattered city; in the Soviet sector, covering the eastern half of the city, Russian tanks and troops, Russian propaganda, and servile German lieutenants had created a totalitarian atmosphere. And their ideology necessarily pervaded the University of Berlin, which the country's rulers turned, most drastically in the social sciences and the humanities, into a haven for conformism and a seedbed of their party line. There was great uneasiness in the western zones of the city, a fear (far from paranoid) that the East Germans, willing puppets of their Soviet masters, might one day invade their neighbor. In fact, only two weeks after our short stay the Stalinist state, called, with a nice sense of the magic of names, the German Democratic Republic, threw up the infamous Wall that dramatized the division and, it then seemed, made it permanent.

The irony of a visit to the Free University was not lost on me. More than a decade earlier, the place had been the cause of a memorable little dispute—memorable at least to me. Around 1950, Franz Neumann, a senior colleague in my department at Columbia, announced that he was on his way to Berlin to do some work for the Free University. As I did in my lowly post as instructor (our elders in the rather grandly named Department of Public Law and Government kept the junior faculty humble lest we begin to nourish the fantasy that someday there might be a tenured post for us), only on a far more exalted level, Neumann taught a course on the history of political thought. Among graduate students and the junior faculty he was a highly respected presence: immensely knowledgeable, commanding a bibliographic range that impressed all his devotees, and benevolently interested in those just entering their professional careers. He made a striking figure: compact, with an eagle's nose, hooded eyes, and a bald head, he looked quite like an idealized Roman emperor. That he needed to wear a hearing aid only seemed to increase his distance from us, but we soon learned that the reserve we perceived was a product of our awe.

In his native Germany, Neumann had been an outspoken trade union lawyer. In May 1933, he barely escaped arrest when a friend who had landed a job with the new regime warned him that he had better leave, the sooner the better. The next morning, he took a plane to London, bringing with him his Marxist Hegelianism, his intimate ties to the Frankfurt School, and his close friend Herbert Marcuse. His bulky study of the Nazi system, *Behemoth,* written after he had moved to Columbia, was then an important text and cemented his reputation among his enthusiastic following. And now this active, consistent anti-Nazi was volunteering to set foot on German soil!

Like my contemporaries at Columbia, I found this hard to fathom. True, Neumann had gathered some notoriety among us with his inflammatory assertion that the Germans were the least anti-Semitic people in Europe. This sally, of which I have often thought since, irritated me, but I was disposed to write it off as a provocation designed to shake us out of our complacent and categorical judgments. To assist in the rehabilitation of the Enemy of Civilization, though, was something else. Filled with righteous indignation, I con-

3

fronted Neumann at the Columbia Faculty Club: "How can you be so sentimental?" His response: "How can *you* be so sentimental?"

It was an inelegant riposte, especially for one so quick-witted as Neumann. But its very lack of originality was like a line drawn in the sand, as if to say, You have your position and I have mine, and there is no way we can reach a compromise, no point in discussing it further. Here were two intelligent academics dangerously near a quarrel, both men of goodwill, both German-born, both émigrés who had had a close call. We let it drop, though I did not stop thinking about the incident.

I did not realize it then, but the episode was evidence that there was no "correct" attitude to take toward the Germans. Individual experiences and private emotions, not all of them directly related to life under the Nazis, justified whatever attitude we took. Some refugees would not buy German cars or appliances, eat in German restaurants, sleep in German hotels, or even concede that the country had ever had a worthwhile culture; a few of them even declined to accept financial restitution offered by the German government from the early 1950s on. I belonged to this camp for some years; I would not even read German, a vengeful stance from which I was obliged to retreat once I entered graduate school in 1946. Many other German Jews who had suffered just as much under the Nazis had no such qualms. My father was of this second party; I remember his Burkean comment— he had never read a word of Burke—that one cannot properly condemn a whole nation. It still rings in my ears. This was the attitude I would slowly, reluctantly, and never completely make my own. Neumann's taunt pursued me: "How can you be so sentimental?"

In 1961 the lesson had not yet quite sunk in. I had left Germany in 1939 as Peter Joachim Israel Fröhlich (the "Israel" courtesy of the Nazis); I returned as Peter Jack Gay,

proud American citizen since 1946. It was a beneficent trans-
formation that I virtually sensed in my bones, as if my American passport made me feel a little taller. The depressing
sense of total vulnerability before implacable Nazi officialdom
had given way to a certain feeling of power. When my parents
and I emigrated, we were literally fleeing for our lives; now I
could stay in Germany as long as it pleased me or, if something rubbed me the wrong way, leave without having to pay
ransom or endure the chicanery at which the Nazis had
proved so inventive. Now I walked on the Wilhelmstrasse,
once the center of government, a street on which in 1938 I
had been forbidden to set foot.

But the moment our rented Dauphine touched German
soil on the Rhine Bridge, I regretted my complicity in this
adventure, an invitation too casually offered and too hastily
accepted. I could have listened to Henry Hatfield's lectures
just as easily in New York—in fact, more easily. Apparently
my American self-confidence was not solid enough to let me
relax among Germans or look forward to seeing the houses
where I had spent my earliest years, the parks where I had
played, the schools where I had recited, the stadiums where
I had cheered. I had returned to Europe three times before:
in 1950, when I spent some six agreeable and productive
weeks in Amsterdam doing research on my dissertation, and
in 1955 and 1958, to visit archives and friends in England and
travel in France and Italy with friends. Each time, I had refused to enter Germany, near though it was.

After that incident at Kehl, I wished I had listened to my
anxiety and my antagonism. Getting out of the car on the
German side to buy marks for dollars in a little kiosk, I had
faced a young woman clerk behind a grille ready to serve me.
She had looked at me coldly, her eyes registering pure hatred
as I handed her my passport. A glance at her had left no
doubt in my mind: murderous anti-Semitism was alive and
flourishing in my native land.

What had happened? Nothing. The clerk dealt with me as she dealt with everyone: correctly and impersonally. If there really was any expression in her eyes, it was surely boredom. I did not know the word *projection* then, nor would it have helped me to thaw out antagonisms so long frozen in my mind. Not even my affectionate travel companion, wrestling with her own feelings, could give me ease. The fact was that this clerk did not hate me; she barely registered my existence. I hated her.

Of course I was freer to hate her than I would have been in the 1930s. As we proceeded on our way, there seemed to be so much, so many, to hate. In 1961 I was thirty-eight, so that the Germans my age had been adolescents under the Nazis, most of the boys enrolled in the Hitler Jugend, most of the girls in the Bund Deutscher Mädel. Those only a little older than I had been adults. Many of them had screamed for Hitler and voted for him, applauded the Nazis' acts of persecution, perhaps cheerfully participated in their killings; many of them had profited from the legalized thievery that had handed over Jewish-owned businesses, Jewish-owned houses, Jewish-owned art collections to "deserving Aryans," had driven musicians, artists, lawyers, physicians, once their fellow citizens, first into isolation and then into exile—always provided that their victims could manage (as we called it) to "get out." Wherever we went, there were Germans: driving their cars, walking their dogs, lounging in cafés, waiting on customers. And they were all speaking German as though nothing had happened, as though their very language had not been permanently contaminated in the Thousand Year Reich.

Their overwhelming presence should not have astonished me: who should surround me in Germany but Germans? And what should they be speaking but German? But such sensible questions were not available to me—not yet. I was at an unstable midpoint along a winding road toward answering my German question, a question that I have not yet completely put to rest and probably never will. Since that first foray in the midsummer of 1961, I have been to Germany many times and for extended visits, made good friends there, done extensive research in libraries and archives, attended conferences, lectured to historians and psychoanalysts and, at the Frankfurt Book Fair, to publishers. Yet even today, when I hear German spoken in an American restaurant or airport, I cannot suppress a slight tensing up and the question, What are they doing here?

Well, I took my German currency from the clerk, climbed back into our Dauphine, and proceeded toward Berlin. A brief stopover in Göttingen to visit a colleague then on leave in Germany only raised the level of tension and fed my paranoia. Rather tactlessly, our host proposed lunch in a large local beer hall, which turned out to be crowded to the walls with elderly fraternity men, many of them wearing their traditional gear. That was bad enough, but when they took to singing their old student drinking songs, Ruth and I had had enough and left. It was poor preparation for the ordeal to come: Berlin was waiting in the distance.

For Ruth and me, four or five uncomfortable days followed. We did not get on with each other, whether in the car or our hotel room; at one point we even discussed turning back. We snapped at each other, bickered in unaccustomed ways. We had had words before and would have words again, but never for a reason so obviously imposed from the outside. It is pointless to assign blame: the provocation of Germany all around us was simply too strong, for Ruth as a newcomer, American-born but from a Jewish Eastern European family, as much as for me, the returning native. Contemporary history raw and ugly had caught up with us.

Worst of all, Berlin proved a letdown. Of course, the city was no longer what it had been in the 1920s and 1930s, when I was a growing boy. The Nazis and Allied bombers had taken care of that. It was not so much that the scars of war, which had ended sixteen years before, were still all too visible. The stalwart working-class women, the memorable *Trümmerfrauen*, who drudged to rehabilitate the city literally stone by stone, had elicited widespread admiration, including mine. But their tireless work had not been enough; there were simply too many wrecks to salvage. After seeing photographs of Berlin in the spring of 1945, a once splendid capital now looking like a gap-toothed derelict, I had expected little else. It was not the physical Berlin of 1961 that further dampened my already exasperated spirits, it was my *experience* of walking through the city. Mindful of Marcel, the protagonist of Proust's great river of a novel, I had anticipated a flood of memories, as though my old neighborhoods would be so many madeleines. But if for him a madeleine dipped in linden tea opened up the world of a long-forgotten past, there were no madeleines for me.

Perhaps nothing illustrates my emotional numbness better than this failure. It reminded me of my inability to weep at my father's death in January 1955. I worked on luring memories from their hiding places, hoping that feelings would wash over me at the dramatic moments I tried to conjure up. Inevitably, it was in walking through the streets where I had spent my childhood that my emotions—and my frustration at my lack of emotions—were most intense. For the first thirteen years of my life, my parents and I lived in one or the other of two apartment houses on the Schweidnitzerstrasse, a street in Halensee. The district, at the western edge of the borough of Wilmersdorf, itself in the western part of Berlin, housed middle-income and lower-middle-income bourgeois only a couple of miles and many thousands of marks from a borough for the gentry like Dahlem.

Schweidnitzerstrasse was unusual in one respect: it was one block long, with some fifteen apartment houses and a small factory. I had played marbles and ball on that street with my contemporaries, for it had little traffic—no buses, no street cars, few automobiles. Right down to the 1930s, few in the middle middle class had cars; my father did have one, an Opel, used largely for business purposes. There was a pub at one corner and a laundry with a huge mangle that greatly impressed me when I was little. For groceries and household items one turned the corner to the Westfälische Strasse. There was one store not far from us, dark, dank, smelly, that sold only potatoes, with a bewildering array of varieties, each in its bin.

Apart from its lilliputian size, our street was of a variety common in the Berlin of my childhood, largely built up before the First World War: its apartment houses were attached side by side, each five stories tall and decorated with an ornate façade; the center segment from the second to the fourth floor jutted forward, giving the living room some added light. A few had balconies that almost destroyed the harmony of the street picture. Almost, but not quite: the restlessness of each building was neutralized by the identical restlessness of its neighbors. Thus Schweidnitzerstrasse made its unpretentious contribution to Berlin's characteristic style, which I liked so much that I believed it must be the natural face of any city.

Like the houses in most other residential districts, those in the Schweidnitzerstrasse were joined at the corners, forming a hollow square in the center, with a spot of grass, on occasion a pitiful misshapen tree, giving the hollow some green, a welcome change from the gray of the stone. During the Depression, out-of-work amateur singers would stand there, addressing the windows in hope of garnering a few pennies. One of their songs, which I must have heard often enough around 1930, was short and doleful, and I can reproduce its melody as well as its text:

> Arbeitslosigkeit, Arbeitslosigkeit,
> Oh, wie bringst du uns so weit!
> Meinen Vater kenn ich nich',
> Meine Mutter liebt mich nich',
> Und sterben mag ich nich', bin noch so jung—

"Unemployment," it went, "unemployment, Oh, how far you have brought us. My father I don't know, my mother doesn't love me, and I don't want to die: I'm still so young."

Now, in 1961, I set up situations that might encourage me to take possession of the life I had once led. But I was checked again and again as I strolled—often alone—through my old streets, past my primary school and my *Gymnasium*. I hunted for landmarks in the neighborhood in which I had grown up. I walked through a park, the Hochmeisterplatz, a two-minute stroll from my first street, to a large, fenced-in playground where at five I had been king of the sandbox and at eight had ridden my bicycle. Across the street from that playground there was a Lutheran church in the Wilhelminian neo-Gothic design, boasting a faceted slender spire and built in the all too familiar dark red brick—not a touch of the pink tinge that can make brick so attractive—which dated the building to the late nineteenth century.

My past, then, was proving to be a mosaic with central pieces missing. I had not reckoned with the fact that one does not arrange for the magic of the madeleine; it comes uncalled or not at all, where and when and how it lists. I discovered in these dismal few days that the images and aroma that rose for Marcel from his cup of linden tea with all the perfume of lost years cannot be forced or prompted. In short, I found that making my way through familiar quarters and looking at familiar buildings produced only a few anemic fragments from my childhood.

Significantly, three of these were horrifying and had frightened me when I was a boy: an idiot who wandered the streets of northern Berlin near my Onkel Siegfried's apartment house, a stunted creature with a gigantic head, awkward gait, and slavering mouth; the torso of a headless chicken that twitched and moved as though it were still alive; the photograph in a magazine of a German soldier dreadfully wounded in the First World War but still living even though half of his face had been shot away. Pleasant memories were much harder to come by.

Candor obliges me to record one episode on this return trip, though, that I experienced as downright bracing. We were driving through Berlin—I was at the wheel—when a policeman waved me over. I had gone through a red light, something I am not in the habit of doing—a tribute to my preoccupation. He asked for my papers, and I handed him my driver's license and passport. As he perused it, he evidently noticed that I had been born in Berlin. He handed back my documents and, in a reasonable, almost paternal tone, suggested that I drive more carefully in the future. My first brush with German authority generated no echoes of the 1930s.

Actually, I felt compelled to acknowledge that the Berlin of 1961 was showing a great deal of animation. Those who had seen it near death, just after the surrender in May 1945, were amazed to see how far the city had come. Its academic institutions were reaching out to universities abroad; the invitation to an American like Henry Hatfield to lecture on so problematic a German writer as Thomas Mann was a token of recovering health. After all, Mann was controversial as an exile who had been unsparing in condemning his homeland, and it was good not to repress but to discuss his meaning for his fellow Germans. We went to hear Hatfield in a large, brand new auditorium and enjoyed it as much as did the students, who drummed their fists on the tables before them as a token of animated approval.

Physically, too, Berlin was working effectively toward a measure of normalcy. Most of the postwar architecture was emergency construction, almost aggressively indifferent to aesthetic considerations, monotonous, listless—utilitarian, in the worst sense of the word. In general, then, post-1945 building in the city, private as much as public, looked like a joyless, unsuccessful facelift, a painted smile. Only a handful of

11

the new buildings were beginning to break with this dreariness. And at least one of the architectural casualties of the war had been turned into an imaginative memorial. Or was it? Such doubts served to undermine my few conciliatory sentiments. High on my list of what I needed to see was the ruin of the Kaiser-Wilhelm-Gedächtniskirche, a grandiose neo-Gothic Protestant church that Germany's last emperor, the flamboyant Wilhelm II, had had built in the early 1890s to commemorate his beloved grandfather Kaiser Wilhelm I. It stood conspicuously in the center of Berlin's western shopping district, at the eastern end of the Kurfürstendamm. This confection, overloaded with heavily tinted glass and servile mosaics celebrating Germany's emperors, had been severely damaged in an Allied air raid, and the city fathers had decided to shore up what was left and, to emphasize its fragmentary remains, place two aggressively modernist constructions next to it.

The torso was a reminder, but in my sour mood I asked myself, a reminder of what? A furious reproach to the Allies for bombing the city so heavily? This cynicism could arise in me at any moment without warning, and that helped to make my first return to Berlin so dismaying. Could it not be, after all, a bitter reproach to the Nazi regime for what it had done to Germans and to Germany? Surely nothing could be a more persuasive indictment of Hitler and his gang than this brooding ruin. Before Germany plunged the world into war in September 1939, every new section opened on the Autobahn, every new stadium or post office constructed in a small town, was credited to Hitler alone: *Das verdanken wir unserm Führer,* read the ubiquitous posters—"We owe this to our leader." But the death and devastation, the famine and humiliation that the war visited on the home front, they too were owed to their Führer—*auch das verdanken wir unserm Führer*—and I could not help but think this a salutary memento.

12

If these ruminations, these sudden shifts in mood, sound inconsistent, they were; my first return to Berlin was an endless attempt to resolve conflicting responses. Yet when all is said, Berlin's display of energy did have its gratifying side for me; I discovered in myself traces of the Berliner I had been before 1933, traces I thought I had forever banished. I recalled more than once that defiant old slogan *Berlin bleibt doch Berlin*—Whatever happens, Berlin remains Berlin—and it had a bracing appeal for me, until it was swamped by my silent hatred.

Unlike other great metropolitan centers, unlike Paris or London, Berlin had been a parvenu among capitals. A small, slowly growing garrison city, headquarters for the impoverished but assertive Hohenzollern dynasty, it had expanded exponentially in the nineteenth century and started to acquire representative cultural institutions: museums, concert halls, opera houses. Late in the nineteenth century there had been a bootless competition between Munich and Berlin as to which was more modern, more civilized; around 1900, it seemed as though Berlin was winning this culture war.

Berlin had long been much despised, which is to say much envied, by other cities. Its humor, blunt, cynical, democratic, busy deflating the bloated and the pretentious, was proverbial. It demystified political rhetoric no less than excessive advertising claims. I remember a slogan used to sell a fire extinguisher that was prominent in my childhood years: *Feuer breitet sich nicht aus, Hast Du Minimax im Haus*—Fire won't spread if you have Minimax at home—which some Berlin wit had undermined with the irreverent commentary *Minimax ist grosser Mist, Wenn Du nicht zuhause bist*—Minimax is a lot of junk when you're not at home. Goethe, who visited Berlin only once, found the "wit and irony" of its denizens quite remarkable; with such an "audacious human type" he decided that delicacy would not get very far and that one

13

needed "hair on one's teeth"—*Haare auf den Zähnen*—a rather baffling tribute that became proverbial because it seemed somehow just right.

Berlin's characteristic speech was quite antiauthoritarian; deflating in its harsh and terse accents, it came naturally to working-class Berliners and was affected by sophisticates who thought linguistic slumming chic. When the operetta composer Paul Lincke extolled Berlin's inimitable air, the *Berliner Luft,* he did not have meteorology in mind but an incontestable mental alertness. And those who agreed with Lincke sensed that he was only putting to music what everyone already knew. Berlin was the kind of city on which travel writers and visiting journalists inevitably bestowed the epithet "vibrant."

This vitality drew heavily on its diverse population, doubtless one reason why Jews felt so much at home there. In 1933, more than 150,000 of them, some 30 percent of the Jews in Germany, lived there. It was a common saying that every Berliner is from Breslau, obviously hyperbole, though it happened to fit my mother, who was born in Breslau and moved to Berlin after her marriage in 1922. In the 1880s Theodor Fontane, poet, historian, critic, novelist, the most interesting German writer between Goethe and Mann, observed that what made Berlin great was its ethnic mix: the offspring of the Huguenots, the provincials who streamed into the city from the surrounding province of Brandenburg, and the Jews. One of these ingredients, the Jews, was sadly absent in 1961. Four years later, when the New School for Social Research in New York honored the social scientists who had fled Hitler's Germany to the United States, Willy Brandt, mayor of West Berlin and an influential politician in the Social Democratic Party, received an honorary degree. And in a moving address—I heard it—he pleaded with his listeners to acquit the youth of Germany, which was, after all, innocent of their parents' crimes, and exclaimed, with the blunt honesty that was his signature: "We miss our Jews."

He had every reason to miss us, though I doubted that his regrets were of vital concern to most Germans. A sizable segment among Berlin's Jews had helped to shape its culture, far out of proportion to their numbers, as scientists, historians, poets, musicians, editors, critics, lawyers, physicians, art dealers, munificent collectors, and donors to museums. Brandt's exclamation of 1965 confirmed the impression I had gathered four years earlier: Berlin's bourgeois culture had lost one of its mainstays and had not replaced it.

It was only to be expected that the Nazis found Berlin a hard nut to crack, even when Goebbels was put in charge of winning it over to the "movement." The city's culture had contributed impressively to what was anathema to the Nazis and their supporters: modernist experimentation with its unconventional theatres, avant-garde novelists and publishers, adventurous newspapers and critics. Their reputation to the contrary, Berlin's Jews were by no means all cultural radicals; many of them, in fact, were solid conservatives in their tastes. Nor were they conspicuous in the city's widely advertised vice. Naturally, I was far too young to partake of the city's forbidden fruit and knew virtually nothing about it. But I early had a taste of its movie palaces, its variety theatres, its sports stadiums, and its bustling streets.

One got around Berlin via an efficient system of subways, elevated trains, and buses, to say nothing of streetcars—we called them *die Elektrische*. I can still hear the screeching noise the cars made, especially around curves, the bright bell the conductor rang warning pedestrians to get out of the way, and the hissing sound that came, occasionally accompanied by little sparks, as the movable rods fixed on the roof of the car made contact with the power line strung overhead. The modern buses that were the streetcars' main competitors were another source of pleasure to me, especially the double-deckers. I found it almost obligatory to climb upstairs and observe the city scene passing beneath me. And nothing could be more thrilling, even a little frightening, than to be on the bus—naturally on the upper deck—as, swaying slightly, it slowly passed through the center space of the Brandenburg Gate; it always looked as though it would scrape against the columns on either side, and it always got through unscathed.

Thus, even though Berlin covered an immense terrain, it seemed very accessible, a fine city for walking. It had made its vastness official in 1920, three years before I was born, by incorporating its proliferating suburbs. But this grab for territory had done no damage to the city's splendid shopping avenues, refreshing parks with comfortable benches, streets with their ever changing incidents, carts from which second-hand dealers sold books. For a walker in Berlin, the favorite west-east artery was the world-famous Kurfürstendamm, with its marvelous wide sidewalks. More than two miles long, it started rather unpretentiously near the street where I lived, but as one walked eastward, one could browse in bookstores, window-shop for clothing, china, even fancy automobiles, and pass movie palaces like the Alhambra (another casualty of the war), to which my parents had taken me, and the Universum, a masterpiece by the brilliant romantic modernist architect Erich Mendelsohn—another emigrant after 1933. Perhaps best of all were the outdoor cafés, where one could sit at leisure, spooning up cake with whipped cream and watching the parade of Berliners on their way. Even before I was ten, I could recognize Berlin's special ambience.

One reason for Berlin's size was that it had been built on a swamp. This meant, until more advanced building techniques unfortunately made skyscrapers practicable, that its profile was low, permitting an expansive canopy of sky overhead. True, it was often gray, but one got used to that. There were a handful of startling exceptions that only underscored the horizontality of Berlin: the skeletal Funkturm, a poor cousin to Paris's Eiffel Tower, dating from the mid-1920s; an office tower for the Borsig locomotive works; and the most dramatic, most uncompromisingly modern building, the ten-story Shell House facing one of the city's canals. With its curved façade and emphatic bands of windows, it was something of a sensation in my childhood. When I saw it again in 1961, it was dilapidated but still standing, a mocking comment on past glories.

All these vistas were secondary to Schweidnitzerstrasse. The apartment in which I spent my early childhood was in No. 10, and even without any concrete memories, I can still sense its roominess and comfort. It even boasted a *Rauchzimmer*—a smoking room—an extra living room that hinted broadly at affluence: the gentlemen retreating to puff on their cigars while the ladies stayed behind to talk of household matters or children and to gossip about unlucky absent ones. For my family, this was largely academic: we entertained rarely, and the smoking room was, I think, never used for its designated purpose. At all events, in the depths of the Depression we moved to far more modest quarters across the street in No. 5. That must have been in 1930.

Our new apartment was acceptable, but only just, a categorical statement that we had come down in the world. We were not exactly poor. We traveled a little, we had money for tickets to soccer games and an occasional movie. Our new apartment had a room for a lodger, with whom, I think, I never spoke (I do recall his name—Bethke—another instance of the caprices of memory), and for a live-in servant, Johanna Hantel. I had a room of my own, a tiny cubicle outfitted with a folding "desk"—really a board covered with linoleum—under my window.

For their part, my parents, without ever complaining, made do with an ingenious arrangement: they turned the largest room into two: a living-dining room, which had a window overlooking the courtyard, and a bedroom for the windowless half. To secure at least a modicum of privacy, they enlisted our two most massive pieces of furniture, a blond moderne armoire placed back-to-back with an ornate buffet, the two acting as a divider. That buffet, a looming mahogany affair with glassed-in turrets at the top sitting on a bulky bottom section with three doors, was to play a certain role in my life.

To relieve some of this drabness, my parents put up several pleasing watercolors of farmyards and half-timbered barns by Josef Menzel—not the celebrated artist Adolph Menzel, but a painter who made a living decorating expensive china plates and cups with well-observed rustic scenes. I have them now. A valuable two-foot-tall porcelain parrot, mainly in brilliant white with yellow and green feathers, which did not survive our emigration, was a reminder of my father's profession—he represented major glass and porcelain manufacturers—and a handsome sight to see. I contributed a bit of color to our apartment with my parakeet, Purzel, a colloquialism for "little fellow," a blue little bird as impudent as they come. It liked to take its food from my lips and interfered with our card games by picking up cards from the table. With its curved beak, I told myself ruefully, it even looked Jewish—at least to readers of the *Stürmer*.

I am pretty sure that I mused about all this—I cannot be certain—as I revisited Schweidnitzerstrasse in 1961. But if memories awoke, they had to contend with a drastically changed scene. I found that neither of my first two apartment houses had survived Allied attentions. No. 5 was a hole in the ground, the site neatly cleaned up, making for a conspicuous gap between its neighbors. And No. 10, too, must have been bombed out of existence or damaged too badly to permit restoration. It had been supplanted by one of those typical post-Nazi buildings of the 1950s, unornamented, looking rather shoddy, as though its life expectancy was limited and perhaps designed to be limited, its flat surfaces broken with an array of tiny balconies on which two, at most three, people could sit to have their afternoon coffee and cake as long as they kept their elbows to themselves.

18

There was yet another apartment house to revisit: in 1936, when, ironically enough, my father was more prosperous than he had been for many years, we moved to Sächsische Strasse 9, a twenty-minute walk northeast of Schweidnitzerstrasse. It was a route I had taken dozens of times to visit my cousins, who lived on the Pariser Strasse, just around the corner from our new, and last German, address. This house, too, proved a casualty. The building and its attached neighbors had been razed to make way for an apartment block set thirty or more feet back from the street (evidently not even the foundations could be rescued) and dressed in the same stuccoed dreariness that had become the signature of the new Berlin.

That, then, was the return of the native. I recognized, dimly then and more clearly later, that if I wanted to take pleasure in Berlin, I would have to reconcile myself to the fact that the old city, my old city, was gone, injured perhaps beyond recovery, wounded in mind probably even more severely than in body. To be sure, I walked past concrete survivals everywhere. Most of the museums, now clustered in East Berlin, had outlived the catastrophe, though looking much the worse for wear. The city's most popular department store, the Kaufhaus des Westens (known only by the affectionate abbreviation KaDeWe) had been rebuilt largely as it had been. The Olympic stadium looked unchanged, and in general the grid of Berlin's streets remained recognizable and happily stripped of the Nazi names by which many of them were known from 1933 on. Some of these continuities were exceedingly mundane but thus all the more riveting: in my boyhood, an optometrist had gained local prominence with a terse slogan: *Sind's die Augen, geh zu Ruhnke*—If it's the eyes, go to Ruhnke. And Ruhnke, complete with slogan, was still in business. But were these survivals a cause for rejoicing or rejection? I did not know and was too torn to find out. All

19

I knew was that the Nazis had poisoned my hometown as they had poisoned so much else, including me. No wonder that when, on August 2, we crossed the border on our return trip to France, my mood drastically improved. After all these years I can still summon up my sigh of relief.

In Training

Some traumas survive everything—the passage of years, the rewards of work, the soothing touch of love, even psychoanalysis. They can be counterbalanced by life, over-borne and outweighed, but an ember remains lodged in one's being to flare up, however fleetingly, at unexpected moments. Not even the most emphatic evidences of success, from domestic happiness to fame, wealth, or the Nobel Prize, can restore completely what was stolen long before. More than a half-century after the collapse of Hitler's Thousand Year Reich, every surviving refugee remains to some extent one of his victims. In recent years, the status of victim has become wildly popular, I know, exploited to elicit sympathy and sustain claims for reparation. I make no such demands. My point is a simple factual one: even the most fortunate Jew who lived under Hitler has never completely shaken off that experience. My mother is a pathetic case in point. A widow for more than twenty years, she moved to a retirement home in 1975 and began in the last two years of her life to suffer occasional bouts of disorientation. She had never been threatened by a Storm Trooper, had never been directly exposed to Nazi violence, but in her errant moments she relived the late 1930s with a horrendous immediacy. She interpreted the occasional loudspeaker announcements in her facility as a signal for a pogrom. She imagined that I had been killed. Then her doctor, whom she trusted, put me on the phone—I had been teaching at Yale for a few years by then—to reassure her that I was alive and quite well. My voice was enough to soothe her anxiety, until the next attack.

I know that there were, and are, thousands of refugees who went through far more and prospered far less, whose wounds have been deeper, more disfiguring, than mine. Some years ago, when I was invited to give a videotaped interview for a program gathering the testimony of "survivors," I complied only under strong protest: I had no right to claim the status of a survivor; I had never been hauled to a concentration camp, nor had my father or mother. I am among the lucky ones.

Yet, ordinary though it may be, I too have a story to tell. It is about one man coping, one mind absorbing, rejecting, transforming the pressures from an increasingly hostile and destructive environment. I shall be talking about politics, but more about psychology—my psychology. This is the kind of story that is usually lost amid the clamor of historic events. And since I spent my early years with my parents in a tightly knit, very small society—I was an only child—I want to start with the way we lived together. Two dates frame this initial exploration: June 20, 1923, when I was born, and January 30, 1933, when Hitler was appointed chancellor of Germany. The first expelled me into life, the second gave my life an ineradicable undertone of mourning. I am writing not to acquit or condemn my little world—that is not my purpose—but to discover as well as I can how my family, quite unknowing, prepared me for the Nazi onslaught. For my first ten years I was, as it were, in training for the catastrophe to come. After all, one brings everything one knows, everything one is, to the trauma when it hits.

My father, in most respects the hero of this story, was born in the village of Podjanze near Kempen in Upper Silesia, the son of an innkeeper. He once told me that although his language at home was German, his first words were Polish. Surrounded as he was by Poles, his memory seems perfectly plausible. But it suggests that the kind of constant interplay between parents and children—talking, singing, reading to them—that we now praise as ideal did not govern his earliest years. This may well explain why my parents, much as they loved me, were not in the habit of reading me stories, which in turn must have encouraged me to read on my own as soon and as much as I could. My father was a self-made man. The local school where he was more or less educated reached only what we would call eighth grade. In fact, at fourteen, with a keen appetite for knowledge, he repeated the highest class to squeeze as much from Kempen's offerings as he could.

After that, most of what he learned he taught himself. He read widely and eclectically and, with his quick intelligence, absorbed much scattered information, enough to develop firm opinions on religion and politics and to give reasons for them. He was a striving bourgeois, a faithful partisan of the German Social Democratic Party (the SPD), attesting not to his radicalism so much as to its respectability. With no training he acquired solid musical tastes: our record collection consisted mainly of operatic arias by world-famous singers like Enrico Caruso. I, too, listened to these recordings, not without profit.

He was a good-looking man, with blue eyes, a straight nose, and slightly wavy hair combed back à la Goethe. He did not, as people said, "look Jewish." As long as I knew him, he was somewhat but never grossly chubby. Though generally healthy and energetic, he was susceptible to repeated, extremely painful kidney stone attacks—this was, I think, his only legacy to me that I have not welcomed. During those episodes, the only painkiller he found effective was morphine; even the drastic remedy of a steaming bath (so hot that I could scarcely bear to touch the water in which he would immerse himself) could not relieve his pain.

23

For all that, he was lively and humorous and liked to massacre snatches of operatic arias with comical, literally nonsensical texts:

> Seht, ich hab's euch gleich gesagt,
> Die Wurst die schmeckt nach Seife—

this from the anvil chorus of *Il Trovatore,* roughly translated, to keep the meter: "Look, I've told you all along: the sausage tastes like soap suds." It was my father, too, who introduced me to an equally nonsensical song, which could be repeated as long as the performer or his audience could bear it:

> Unrasiert, und fern der Heimat,
> Fern der Heimat, unrasiert—

"Unshaven and far from home, far from home unshaven." He also enjoyed misapplying a line of grave poetry grossly inappropriate to the occasion: when one of us urgently needed to go to the bathroom, he would recite the penultimate line from the *Erlkönig,* Goethe's grim ballad about a dying child: *erreicht den Hof mit Müh' und Not*—"he barely manages to reach the courtyard." He was cheerfully descending to my boyish level.

My mother's style was a vivid contrast to my father's spirited ways, though they beautifully complemented each other. Born in Breslau in 1900, she was eight years younger than my father, an age difference that German folk wisdom called ideal for marriage: in 1922, at the time of her wedding, she was half as old as my father plus seven. Whatever the truth of this pseudoscientific lore, it applied to my parents. I never heard a cross word, never saw a cross look between them. The product of a genteel girls' school, my mother played the piano passably and with evident enjoyment. She was petite and very slight, with lovely eyes, the undisputed beauty in the family. Her health was uncertain, however; consistently underweight, more than once she resorted to a clinic to fatten up. Then, in the 1930s, she contracted tuberculosis. More than that, she was plagued by psychosomatic illnesses, which left their mark on me.

None of her fragility kept my mother from being active in her world. For years she spent part of the day clerking in her sister's notions store, competently selling thread, buttons, or stockings. And she ran our household efficiently enough, though she was not a distinguished cook. For years my parents would spend much of Sunday morning in bed reading the newspaper while a chicken was cooking away on the stove. The inevitable result: excellent chicken soup and dry, cardboardlike chicken. Because I was a poor eater, these failures did not trouble me in the least. I do recall one amusing episode: one day my mother ventured to make potato dumplings, a delicacy she had not tried before. But her dumplings disintegrated, and try as she did to rescue them with a skimmer, all that came up were tiny fragments. Not that my father reproached her—that was not his way with her. And I did not know enough to mind.

My father's four siblings played a relatively minor role in my life. His two sisters, Esther and Recha, lived in Breslau, and we saw them only occasionally. My Tante Esther was married to Moritz Jaschkowitz, a stocky man with a prognathous jaw, involved in some sort of business. She had handsome, delicate features and stunning long blonde hair: it is one of the appalling ironies of my family history that she, whom the Nazis later murdered in an extermination camp, was assigned the role of Germania in a school play. As I recreate her in my mind, and as surviving photographs confirm, she habitually wore a tragic expression, the corners of her mouth pulled down. I don't think her marriage was happy, but I liked Onkel Moritz because he taught me skat, the German version of bridge—first, if I remember rightly, with a deck featuring great composers rather than the customary royalty. I think he must have been away from home a good deal of the time, no doubt playing that game with his cronies. As for my Tante Recha, an inconspicuous figure in my life,

I knew that she had a son but no husband, an interesting fact that nobody ever bothered to explain to me. She, too, ended up in the gas chambers.

The others would be more fortunate. Of my father's two brothers, only one, Onkel Max, impinged on my life. The other, Onkel Siegfried, known as Siege, lived some hundred miles away in Magdeburg and rarely showed himself in Berlin. His marriage to a gentile woman did not trouble my parents in the least, but I think we did not make him particularly welcome. I do not remember why, but I know that I was disgusted by the wet kisses he implanted on me with his sensually curved lips—this was not my parents' manner, or mine.

I found Onkel Max far more likable. Unlike his brothers, he was spare, with sharply etched features. He lived in Berlin, and for several years my father gave him a job in his small company. This was a tribute more to my father's familial feeling than to my uncle's competence. Onkel Max seemed to be something of a problem, known for not working hard and for his inability to keep a job. But I liked him—children naturally value adults who are good to them—because he told me stories, something that no one else did. I have a tantalizing memory of having been told that he once stole my father's tuxedo. This is one of those Wodehousian episodes I would give much to recover, but like so much else in my past, this moment has been swallowed up in the quicksands of amnesia.

My mother's siblings were far more present to me. For one thing, we were yoked together by closely twisted family ties. Samuel Fröhlich, born in 1885, was my father's uncle, and his wife, Tante Hedwig (known as Hede), was my mother's oldest sister. In fact, my parents had met at Onkel Samuel and Tante Hede's wedding. They lived near us, even nearer from 1936 on than before. Their two sons, Hanns, three years older than I, and Edgar, my age, were my constant companions. We would have been close even without the Nazis' coming to power, for, like many middle-class families, we lived much with one another. But as the noose tightened around Germany's Jews and we grew more and more isolated from the outside world, our intimacy grew.

While much united the two Fröhlich families, what divided us was far more interesting. The quarrels and reconciliations among the other Fröhlichs, the disparity between their religious professions and religious beliefs, provided me with some crucial lessons. They were a quartet that often played out of tune. Tante Hede was all business and activity, Onkel Samuel pasty-faced, choleric, and insignificant in family councils. In that couple, Tante Hede, with her formidable energy and need to be in command, was necessarily the leader; her husband, always too heavy and growing more flabby with the years, was no match for her. The story went that in her younger days, when, as photographs show, she approached what one might call stern good looks, she had been in love with a man who was killed in the war. Whatever the substance of this family tale, she married when she was uncomfortably close to thirty, barely evading the dreaded fate of the spinster. She seems to have given up on whatever attractiveness was naturally hers; certainly by the time she entered my life, what she lacked in looks she made up in decisiveness. Her motto was, "Unfortunately, I am always right," and she meant it.

One of my mother's brothers, Onkel Siegfried Kohnke, a beloved presence in my life, was very different. (His name calls for two comments. It is significant that two of my uncles were called Siegfried. Such names, partly traceable to Wagner, were not uncommon—my mother's first name, Helga, was Nordic if it was anything. If such aliases had been intended to camouflage a Jewish background, they soon proved counterproductive: only Jews, the word went, really liked those Teutonic first names. And Kohnke became the subject of a family joke: how much, the question went, did the Kohnkes have to pay for the appendix *ke*, which made the name sound less Jewish than "Kohn"? It was the kind of joke the

Nazis made even less funny than it had been before them.) A small manufacturer, Onkel Siegfried lived in Gesundbrunnen, a lower-middle-class neighborhood in northern Berlin, particularly familiar to me because it was near the Herthaplatz, the stadium in which my favorite soccer team, Hertha Berliner Sports Club (known as B.S.C.), played its home games. Unfortunately for him, Onkel Siegfried was good-natured to the point of gullibility. Perhaps the term *passive* describes him best. He allowed people to cheat him without taking action, and he was magnanimous far beyond the average, even beyond reason. I remember pestering him about a specially constructed radio that he had given me—I can still see it, with its row of many buttons—and that, like an overindulged child, required constant attention. Onkel Siegfried would drag it around to repairmen as though he had nothing better to do. And, much like my father, he enjoyed puns and misapplied quotations from the classics. Referring to streets in his neighborhood amply supplied with bars where drunks would stumble along the sidewalk, he would intone: *Ihr naht Euch wieder, schwankende Gestalten*—You approach once again, wavering shapes. Surely in the opening line of his dedication to *Faust,* Goethe had been alluding to distant and uncertain memories rather than to intoxicated humans.

This amiability dictated Onkel Siegfried's life. For years he had been carrying on an affair with a woman who was in constant ill health. We almost never saw her; my vague memory of her is of a solemn face with glasses and high cheekbones that made her look like a tight-lipped, cruel schoolmarm. When her health deteriorated to the point that the end seemed imminent, Onkel Siegfried married her in a deathbed ceremony, only to have her recover enough to live on for twelve years, without, I think, giving my uncle much pleasure. Why does life so often turn out like the plot of a cheap novel?

The difference between Onkel Siegfried and his brother

Onkel Willy was striking. A man with a saturnine expression, balding head, and dapper mustache, Onkel Willy was fond of living well and constantly involved with glamorous women, more than one of whom he married. He was given to rages against members of his family, especially his sister Hede, but never against my mother, whom he treated (as did the others) like a precious, rather fragile creature. When these quarrels erupted—they did not cease and were carried on by mail after Onkel Willy had emigrated—my father was the mediator to whom even that proud man would appeal. I have kept one of these letters in which he says of his older sister: "If a monument to wickedness is ever erected, it will bear Hede's features." This uninhibited vehemence was alien to me and to my parents.

But Onkel Willy was liberal with me. I have a dim recollection (or did my parents tell me the story later?) that when I was around five, he bought me an expensive toy that I had coveted: a car big enough to hold me, with pedals that made the contraption move when I stepped on them. Even if this is not a faithful memory, it testifies to my feelings for him in those days. And an afternoon I spent with Onkel Willy in his bachelor apartment in 1932, when I was nine—the last year of the Weimar Republic—remains fixed in my mind and even on my palate. His place was on the top floor, with a large balcony overlooking one of Berlin's most spacious avenues, the Kaiserdamm. When we heard marching rhythms to martial-sounding band music, we stepped onto the balcony to be greeted by a reassuring sight in a city in which unruly Nazi Storm Troopers had been all too visible: a parade of the Reichsbanner Schwarz-Rot-Gold, an anti-Nazi paramilitary organization that had incorporated the colors of the Weimar Republic—black, red, gold—into its name. This was one of the first sources of possible dissent that the Nazis stamped out with brutal dispatch once they took power.

That is not all that remains to me from this day, crowded as it was with impressions. The most startling feature of Onkel Willy's large living room was a row of mirrors that took up the length of a wall. By pressing on a knob, one could move two or three of the panels to reveal a clothes closet and a small bathroom. It was as though Onkel Willy had given me a precious hint of an elegance that was miles removed from my own rather shabby living quarters. One other treat, though, did not end happily. Onkel Willy fed me a delicacy that I had never eaten—never even heard of—before: pilchards, herring bathed in tomato sauce. I found them delicious, ate too many of them, and vomited them all up. I might have anticipated that result: the pilchards went with the apartment, the balcony, the mirrored wall—in short, the excess that my Onkel Willy incarnated and that I found supremely attractive. I have never eaten pilchards since.

Finally, there was my "American" Onkel Alfred, who with his family literally saved our lives. Closest in age and temperament to my mother, he had two passions: chess and the violin. I have the impression that he played both creditably. Among my treasures is a charming photograph of him at ten or eleven, in a sailor suit and holding a violin, as my mother, in a checked jumper and with a ribbon in her hair, turns around from her piano to face the photographer. A captious spirit (don't count me among them!) might say that Onkel Alfred was unbusinesslike to a degree, given to hypochondria, and somewhat pedantic. I remember his letters to me from the United States, in which he would, like a latter-day Henry James, set off colloquial expressions with quotation marks as though to distance himself from the informalities he was allowing himself. But these were superficial eccentricities. He was decency and loyalty itself, and when it counted, when we desperately needed him, extremely effective.

It was through chess that Onkel Alfred met Aunt Grace, the incomparable woman he married. One day, it must have been in 1921 or 1922, he was playing chess at the house of an older Breslau friend and encountered a young American woman on a visit from the small town of Quincy, in the Florida panhandle. Her father, an emigrant from Germany, had settled there a half-century before. Peddling saws, hammers, and nails, he prospered over the years. Aunt Grace was well educated, civilized, and thoughtful—qualities that do not always go together. She was fond of music and filled the house with books. The lifelong victim of insomnia, she made as little of it publicly as she could. I have never met anyone who was so easy to love. Aunt Grace and Onkel Alfred were married in July 1923.

I know nothing about their courtship, but it spawned yet another mild family legend: she spoke no German and he no English, the perfect starting point for a happy marriage. What matters most—it saved our lives—is that after they married, they decided to settle in the United States. It was a rational decision: in the early days of the Weimar Republic, the economic situation in Germany was dire, and my Onkel Alfred had no particularly salable skills. So he went from Breslau, a prominent urban center rich in music and chess players, to a tiny Florida town where there was very little of one and less of the other. Quincy offered Onkel Alfred virtually no outlets for his interests. Fortunately, Aunt Grace proved a real companion for him. The couple would drive more than a score of miles to Tallahassee for concerts and recitals. At home, he practiced his violin and even found some chess partners. After I came to the United States, I played chess with him by mail, but that correspondence gradually faded: I was simply no match for him.

This, then, in addition to my cousins, about whom I will speak often, was the cast of characters that will make its appearance in the pages that follow. But I am not writing a family history: the principal actor of the piece will be myself.

My parents were modern liberals. This meant, for one thing, that they were restrained with each other in public. I do not remember ever seeing them hug or kiss, even when the public consisted of just their only child. Certainly they were, as I have said, a completely devoted pair. No kisses, but also no hard words. They were a handsome couple. My mother would have been more handsome still if her face had not often seemed so tense; as people then used to say, she was nervous. My father was the more expressive of the two, but I have no inkling that he ever bullied his wife. The two simply agreed on the important as on the small things in life. On the rare occasions when they did not—my mother, all anxiety about long trips, was uneasy about emigrating—my father, with good reasons on his side, would win out. When he died in January 1955, at the early age of sixty-two—we were living in Denver then—several fellow refugees urged my mother, who was not yet fifty-five, to marry again. She dismissed their well-meant suggestion with scorn.

They were modern liberals, too, in that they did not yell at me or spank me. My father once recalled for my benefit a single incident that had not registered with me but evidently gave him some trouble in retrospect: when I was little more than two, walking with him and my Tante Esther, I got bored or tired and begged to be carried. When my father proved unwilling to oblige, I started a sit-down strike, which he broke with a spot of corporal punishment. This was so exceptional an incident that he could bring it to mind years later. My household was the proverbial ideal world in which my parents spoke softly and needed no stick. I almost never argued with them, but then I found very little to argue about. I disliked my bath, a regular feature of Fridays, but my resistance was feeble, almost a predictable gambit. Of evenings, whenever I tried to prolong my day, my father would remind me, without raising his voice, that it was bedtime. And I would go.

I must have been a most tractable boy. One day when I was still very little, my parents decided to hire a live-in servant who combined the duties of a maid with those of a nanny. In the latter capacity, she apparently discovered that I was spoiled. It had been my habit to go to sleep with the door of my room open to the hall, which was lighted. The

first night my new educator turned off the light, and the next
night she closed my door. All this with no protest from me.

If there was one principle that governed my upbringing it
was consistency. My parents established a sort of unwritten
code for me, and at least consciously it never occurred to me
to question it: was it not sensible and benign? They never
said so, but we three concluded a tacit compact: I was to be
honest with them and well behaved, and they would reason
with me. My father took some pride in the fact that his actions did not belie his maxims. He made fun of Onkel Samuel
for exploding at his sons' misdeeds, threatening to withhold
their allowance for a month and to break every bone in their
body, only to retreat ignominiously from his preposterous
threats a few hours later. If I were ever to threaten to break
every bone in your body, my father told me, I would do it.
This sounds chilling, but he did not think for a moment that
he would ever lose his temper so disgracefully or that I would
ever give him the slightest cause to do so.

I should add that not only were there few punishments
in my house, there were also copious rewards: going to soccer
games with my father or to a movie with my parents, or visiting my cousins to play cards. My parents bought me books,
and mother and I would haunt the local public library (in the
basement of my primary school, I think) in an attempt to
assuage my appetite for reading, far greater than my appetite
for food. My agenda was large and catholic, and prominently
included stories of adventure, true or invented. Like every
German boy of that time, I read volume after volume of the
adventures of Karl May in America and the Near East. But
I also raced through Hugh Lofting's series on the travels of
Dr. Dolittle and his talking animal companions, of course in
German translation, which was literal or phonetic—the two-
headed Push-Me, Pull-You became the Stoss-Mich, Zieh-
Dich, and the clever duck became Göb-Göb in German. I
swallowed accounts of polar explorations, with Fridtjof Nan-
sen my clear favorite, even though—or perhaps because—he

never reached his goal, and his heroism and intelligence had appealing touches of pathos to them. I read children's versions of the *Iliad*, taking sides as though the Trojan War had been a sporting event, and, with even more delight, the *Odyssey*, whose hero, as strong as he was wily, was my man.

One precocious career choice was quickly stifled. For some months, when I was eight or nine, I wanted to grow up to be an astronomer. But Onkel Willy ruined this ambition by telling me that not long before, an astronomer in his observatory open to the night sky had been found frozen to death, an occupational hazard I had not counted on.

But the Mohrenkopf trumped all these pleasures. A ball of sponge cake with a bit of custard in its innards and covered with chocolate glaze, it was sublime eaten straight but even more so piled high with whipped cream. This was my great bonus: every day I had been good, which meant every day, I would trundle over to a nearby bakery and get my treat. After six decades I still literally salivate at the memory, like one of Pavlov's dogs.

But while I had much to enjoy at home and much that I did enjoy, some of my most deeply etched early memories are of sickness. I had all the usual childhood diseases in fairly rapid succession, around the ages of five and six: mumps, measles, the lot. My tonsils were an indefatigable enemy, easily enlarged and inflamed, but fortunately our family physician, Dr. Peter Wolffheim, Onkel Peter to me, a genial practitioner and no sadist, vetoed having them taken out.

No wonder my recollections focus on beds. Here I am in my parents' bed, shivering with flu, covered with as many feather comforters as can be piled on to make me sweat and break the fever. Or, a particularly hateful variant, I am wrapped in a wet, cold sheet to achieve the same result. Here I am again in my parents' bed, this time sitting up, my head hurting badly as I tilt it to the right as far as I can to have the doctor, or perhaps my mother, pour a small amount of heated oil into my left ear. I have an ear infection, as I often did, and the heat is supposed to open the eardrum and let the pus dribble out. When the remedy works, the eardrum pops with a palpable, almost lascivious noise, instantly leaving me free of pain.

Now it is 1928; I can see my mother in bed, looking weepy and drawn, more sick than sad. Her father, my grandfather, whom I hardly knew, has just died. And a year later, in the spring of 1929—I am in first grade—I am in my own bed with the shades drawn to keep me in semidarkness; I see a man standing at the open door of my room. This is Onkel Alfred, on a visit from Quincy, but he has been forbidden to enter because I have been struck with scarlet fever, a highly infectious disease, and for the remainder of my uncle's visit I am unfortunately in quarantine.

I suspect that my parents arrived at their progressive way with me because they, too, had been treated gently and now sowed what they had reaped. Besides, their liberalism was much in vogue in the early 1920s. Not that my parents were fashionable people; they were sound, if at times financially strapped, bourgeois. But the fashion suited their temperament and their experience. My mother's parents had owned a stationery store in the heart of Breslau, on the Ring, and had given her the kind of bland schooling that the daughters of the prosperous middle class usually received. Her accomplishments, as I have said, included playing the piano, and I can still hear her playing Chopin with some facility. Accordingly, I too was sent to a piano teacher at an early age, and I visualize a neat old lady who received me in her apartment not far from ours. I particularly remember admiring a reproduction on her living room wall, *The Concert*. It showed rapt listeners, one with his eyes closed, another looking up to heaven, their hands folded in prayerful attention. This picture somehow suited my parents' way of life, just as Chopin and Caruso did. In sum, at home everything was as it should have been and would have continued to be but for a historical catastrophe when I was nine and a half.

My parents, then, did not spank me because it was not their style, and because, as I have admitted, I was too predictably obedient to require much if any punishment. Among our surviving photographs there is one taken when I was about three that seems to be emblematic of my irreproachable and untimely virtue. I am plainly posing as I kneel on a chair, all dressed up in what look like a brand-new shirt and shorts, sporting a crisp haircut with every hair neatly in place. I am thoughtfully staring at a box filled with what look like poker chips; an expressionless teddy bear almost as large as I am sits in the background, watching the display. As I leaf through the photo album that my mother began to assemble soon after I was born, I happen upon a caption in which she notes that when I was four and a half months old, my parents took me to Breslau to show me off to my maternal grandparents; on the train, she adds, I was well-behaved—*artig*—on the way to Breslau and "almost well-behaved" on the return trip. It is a well-meant compliment that I cannot read now without a pang of uneasiness. To have been "artig" so persistently, starting at so early an age, was bound to invite trouble later. To be so good had to be a screen for being afraid of being very bad.

I do not doubt that in their undemonstrative way my parents cherished me. In my mother's photo album I appear over and over from my first days on, smiling, crying, yawning, having just shat into my diaper, a form of self-expression that my mother recorded with a homemade euphemism. The first set of photographs shows me at eighteen days ("Peterle is already laughing"); the second captures me at age one month and two days, and so into my future at irregular but frequent intervals. Small, amateurish, often sadly faded pictures show me in my mother's arms, or being held by my father, an uncle, or a grandparent, or alone on the potty. In the captions, my mother's names for me are fond diminutives: Peterle or Peterchen. When my parents arrive in Breslau to parade me around, there is, in my mother's note, "great joy." Through all these years and later, my father called me Spatzi, little sparrow, a nickname that never grew stale for me.

Yet my two earliest memories point in opposing directions. They have bravely struggled to the surface of my mind through the thick fog of forgetfulness. I am in a hotel with my parents, perhaps on the way to a family visit or a spa. There has been a power failure which has cut off the water supply, and my parents, knowing how much I dislike carbonated water, have put a glass of seltzer on a dresser to let the bubbles escape so that I may drink in comfort. But then: I am at home, there are guests in the living room listening to a humorous record played on our phonograph. It is of a trumpeter trying to perform a solo and hitting a sour note; he tries again and again, only to repeat the same mistake at the same place, and someone begins to laugh at the trumpeter's discomfiture. This was known as a *Lachplatte,* a laughing record, but because I am too small to pronounce every letter clearly and have trouble with *p*, I call it a "Lachlatte," which must have amused the assembled company all the more. My parents well know that I cannot abide this record and break down in tears whenever it is played, whether from premature compassion or for some other reason. Still, they play it again. Balance sheet: one act of kindness, one of callousness. If this were baseball, it would be a sensational, never-yet-heard-of batting average. But this was not baseball.

Truth-telling, I have intimated, was the proof and test of my parents' liberalism. Some beneficent legends were exempt from this ideal: I was, as a small boy, much afraid of thunderstorms and soon learned, in order to control my responses, to count the time elapsing between the lightning and the thunder, with each three seconds counting as one kilometer away. My parents told me not to worry: it was the gods bowling in the heavens above. But apart from such emergency measures, honesty was the only policy. In fact, I regarded my relation to my parents as unique, and uniquely fortunate. I

fancied it to be a kind of partnership, an illusion partly created by my parents' treating me as more adult than my
growing frame and developing mind could easily accommodate. One main reason I kept this illusion alive was surely
the noisy way that my cousins were being brought up, always at a fancied risk of having their bones broken. All this
Sturm und Drang made my own household seem tranquil, a
veritable idyll of infinite purity, far superior to life in all other
families.

In this atmosphere of openness, my single childhood lie
stands out like a stain of red wine on a white tablecloth. For
lesser beings inured to dishonesty, this would have been a
trivial incident. For me it was a puzzling and unnerving shat-
tering of a smooth surface, not at all understood then and
not completely understood now. I am—how old? six? certainly no more than seven. My mother has sent me out to a
neighborhood store to pick up a few necessities and, as usual,
handed me money to cover my purchases. While I am in the
store, I see a ball of sturdy twine that I suddenly crave. I have
been flying kites lately, and this cord looks strong enough to
withstand the sharpest breeze. I buy it along with the rest
and, not reporting it, keep the string to myself. My mother,
going over the change I hand her, finds some money missing
and asks me about it. A novice at lying, I confess instantly.
Why steal what my mother would have been glad to buy
for me? The string, after all, cost only a few pennies. That
night, in disgrace, I eat in the kitchen rather than with my
parents.

What was it? A child's impetuosity seeing only the immediate reward? Impatience with my perfection? More telling: sheer rage or perhaps a masochistic need to be found
out and punished? Much of this sounds far-fetched, but it
occurs to me in this connection that I was rather accident-
prone: once, getting off a streetcar in front of my cousins'
apartment house, I was hit by a car passing between the
halted streetcar and the sidewalk, an accident that mobilized

all my family as I lay decorously on a couch, no consequences
but a headache.

On another occasion, leaving a movie house on the Kurfürstendamm I barely escaped being hit by another car. I
remember that movie well; it was a film version of Franz
Lehàr's operetta *The Land of Smiles,* starring that great melt-
ing tenor Richard Tauber—he, too, would have to emigrate
on "racial" grounds. There are good reasons, I think, for recalling that film with such poignant clarity. Tauber portrays
an aging Japanese suitor who gives up the young woman he
loves to a younger, more eligible rival. I can still sing fragments of his pathetic love song, as many can do in English
translation:

> Dein ist mein ganzes Herz,
> Wo Du nicht bist, kann ich nicht sein—

"Yours is my heart alone; where you are not, I cannot be."
And, even more affecting to this young boy:

> Aus Apfelblüten einen Kranz,
> Leg ich Dir, Lieblichste, zu Füssen
> In einer Mondnacht, im April—

"I place a wreath of apple blossoms, loveliest one, at your
feet, on a moonlit night in April." Heady stuff, no doubt, but
what spoke to me most distinctly was the aria in which
Tauber laments the artifices governing his deeply repressed
culture: "Always smiling and always cheerful," he sings, "but
what goes on inside is no one's business."

But whether directed against myself or others, what place
should rage of any kind have in my young life? Surely if there
ever was a boy who had no cause for it, I was that boy. One
thing is certain—I have no doubt on this point—I was never
consciously angry at my parents. Then I recall the bicycle
incident and begin to wonder. In Berlin of the 1920s, children
riding the smallest bicycles were permitted to use the sidewalk. Happily I would ride my bike from one end of Schweid-

nitzerstrasse to another. But one day, chugging along, I noticed an old lady slowly walking toward me. I had plenty of time to stop or to swerve around her; instead I ran into her and she fell. Whatever happened afterward I never found out; my parents could be relied upon to smooth things over. I do not even think that they forbade me the bicycle.

I have become convinced that my closing in on my victim expressed some unconscious rage, a hostile feeling that I had learned to repress. The myth of perfection by which my parents and I lived, a veritable *folie à trois,* was too precious to be tarnished by the reality of mixed feelings that troubled other, more ordinary mortals. Repression? Things that do not happen are notoriously hard to track down, but everyone knows that the dog that did not bark in the night gave Sherlock Holmes the clue he needed. The absence of all anger at my parents must arouse suspicion. In educating me, especially in making me the good boy I was, they necessarily had to deny me many of my wishes. For me, as for everyone else, being fitted for life involved one deprivation after another. Just as my parents gently forced me to go to bed when they determined it was time to go, so they taught me, just as gently, how to share a piece of cake with other children at a birthday party. And I took all this cheerfully, without a touch of resentment? Was I, alone of all children in the world, spared oedipal affections and hatreds? I now see the old lady I may have sent to the hospital as a hapless substitute for targets I dared not even dream about.

One other episode of these early years confirms, I think, that I was a far angrier boy than I could have imagined. I attended primary school from 1929 to 1933, but even though I have saved a group photo of my class and teachers taken on an excursion in 1930 (I have no trouble recognizing myself), I have only a single memory of these four years—a fistfight with a classmate during which I broke the knuckle of the little finger on my right hand. This gives me no reason to boast about my prowess as a fighter: the break came as my antagonist suddenly turned his head so that I hit the hardest part of his skull. But that is not the point. The point is that of this long stretch in my childhood, only one act of rage has survived in my mind. An accident? There are no such accidents in the universe that Freud has discovered for us.

Anger long remained a confused category to me. Many years later, during my training analysis, I told my analyst that I never knew whether my mother was angry at me for some reason or was only feeling ill. In retrospect, I know that I mistook the latter for the former, and I confess that I value this conjecture as an important insight for me. My mother, in addition to her physical ailments, was troubled by certain neurotic inhibitions of which, I think, she rarely spoke, but which I acquired through some mysterious process of osmosis and which lasted until puberty, and even for some time after that. At a movie or the theatre, my mother would sit anxiously on the aisle, afraid that something untoward could happen to her. I did not directly imitate her behavior, but her tensions became mine.

That my mother loved me as much as she could seems to me beyond doubt, but her ability to give voice to her affection for me was compromised by her anxieties and her ailments. It took me many years to recognize what her partial invalidism had done to me. Children, I discovered, are likely to take their parents' adversity, whether manifested as quarrels or illnesses, onto their own shoulders and blame themselves for whatever disrupts domestic harmony. No concrete memories attach to my problematic responses to my mother. I have been accused of being thin-skinned; the first to say so, in fact, was my mother, who charged me with lacking a sense of humor. If this is true, here is where it started.

Such things are admittedly hard to pin down. A much later memory may offer a clue. It must have been around 1944, when I was an undergraduate at the University of Denver. From my arrival in the United States three years before, I had been passionately eager to perfect my English, and I browsed through modern fiction, quickly growing infatuated with one writer after another. In my early days in Denver, in 1941 and 1942, haunting the public library, I could not distinguish between Upton Sinclair and Sinclair Lewis, but that time of sheer ignorance soon passed. My first idol, whose style I copied in several unpublished—and unpublishable—stories, was Ernest Hemingway: those tough short sentences! that laconic dialogue! "The Killers" was my favorite. But after a time, I graduated from what I came to see as Hemingway's forced virility to subtler exemplars. Having come across E. B. White and bought a remaindered collection of his columns, *One Man's Meat,* I suddenly had a very different literary model. I thought it essential to introduce my mother to my new love, so one day I read a paragraph of E. B. White's to her. My mother's English was imperfect but quite serviceable, and she listened patiently. But she did not respond at all. No smile, no frown, no praise, no cavils—nothing. It seems childish of me to have been so dismayed by her unresponsiveness, and it *was* childish, quite literally. Had I needed her less, I would have understood that she was after all not a student of English literature. If there was a failure in that episode, it was mine. But whoever's fault it was, it throws a long shadow back to my childhood.

It seems brutally unfair to my mother, but to this day she remains entrenched in my superego; she makes me uncomfortable. She almost never appears in her own voice, but I recognize her in all her disguises. It is my mother who reminds me that I have left a chore partly unfinished or have done what I should have left undone. I have been clumsy, she tells me quietly, I have been forgetful, I have been selfish. Not that she did not believe in me; once we had lived in the United States for some time, and while I was working at the humblest jobs, she never failed to remind me that I was not cut out to be a shipping clerk forever but was intended for greater things. To be a respected and influential columnist like Walter Lippmann, she thought, would suit my talents.

And she trusted me: when I told her in 1958 that I wanted to marry a divorced woman with three young daughters, she offered none of the expected objections and was instantly ready to include these four new beings in my life within her love for me. If I chose such a woman, was her reasoning, she must be all right. Yet for all that, she has left traces in me less of smiling approval than of soft-spoken censoriousness.

In a well-known formulation, Freud speaks of the return of the repressed. Long-harbored emotions which to all appearances had died away vault to the surface and demonstrate by their headlong rush to expression that they had been there all along, but buried so deeply that their reappearance and their energy must seem astonishing. This is how my childhood rage, the rage I thought I had never felt, overpowered me in a telephone booth in Denver's Union Station in early September 1954. Hardly a dignified setting, but the unconscious makes its own choices about where and when it decides to break out.

Ever since graduating from the University of Denver in 1946 and moving to graduate school at Columbia, I had made a habit of visiting my parents between teaching terms or late in the summer. By 1954 my father was visibly failing. His health had not been satisfactory for several years, and he had retreated to his easy chair by the window in the living room. From that vantage he could see the entrances of several ground-floor apartments, and he would comment on who was coming to the house and who was leaving it. His poor circulation was growing noticeably worse, and I found it heartbreaking to see this interesting and alert human being shrinking to a mere shadow of the self I had known and loved so well.

It so happened that after many vicissitudes my Onkel Willy had landed in Denver, much older but still feisty after years of wandering through South Africa and Latin America. With a new wife, Gertrude, a highly competent businesswoman, he had built up a prosperous store, featuring high fashions imaginatively selected and reasonably priced. In their euphoria, though, Onkel Willy and his wife paid little attention to my parents, an indifference that my father would have laughed off in earlier years but now found insulting. My mother, only too aware of my father's condition, asked me to call Onkel Willy and suggest that he show more consideration by at least inquiring occasionally how my father, clearly a dying man, was faring. I made my call from the station and put the case as politely as I could. In response, I got a blast from my uncle. He accused me of having been in Denver for six days—six days!—before getting in touch with him (true but irrelevant) and called me names (unwarranted and quite as irrelevant). And then the dam broke. I cannot reconstruct my language, but it was rich and rare. What I do remember precisely is that when I got on the train and sank into my seat I was breathing hard and my pulse was pounding.

It was a great moment of liberation, but not the panacea I had hoped for. In my fond imagination I had thought of rage as a fixed quantity. The more I released, the less would be left. But it soon appeared that my fury was being fed by a subterranean stream that continuously refilled the reservoir I thought I had emptied. There was a great gain for me that day, no doubt, but because I had attacked the wrong target, or at least a peripheral target, the eventual benefits were limited. The roots of my anger went deep, into my early childhood.

Practically the only thing that worried my parents about me as a young boy was that I was a poor eater. After 1933, when I went to gymnasium, I would sometimes throw away my lunch rather than eat it, but the problem had arisen far earlier. My father should have been a model to me in this: he ate whatever he was served, and very quickly. But I went my own perverse way. I developed some strange superstitions about food—I have no idea where I picked them up: if you swallow a cherry pit, you will get appendicitis; when you eat a banana, you must not drink water afterward, or some unspecified ailment will afflict you. There were many foods I simply refused to touch, and neither cajolery nor sarcasm would persuade me to enlarge my skimpy catalogue of edibles. Usually so kind and patient, my father would cite an old proverb, more in resignation than in indignation: *Was der Bauer nicht kennt, frisst er nicht*—A peasant won't gulp down what he doesn't know. My mother, a little less patient, would look at me as I listlessly chewed on something I did not like: "Don't choke like that all the time!" I don't suppose it occurred to her—or to me—that she of all people was far from well placed to criticize my eating habits. Nothing helped. Once a year, though, on my birthday, I got my dream dinner, and I would eat all of that: pot roast with cream sauce, red cabbage, and mashed potatoes.

In the course of time, my parents developed several schemes to improve my appetite. At the end of the 1920s, they hired a new maid, Johanna Hantel. She came from a sizable peasant family settled in a tiny village, Kümmritz, some fifty miles south of Berlin. Her four brothers, her parents, and one venerated grandparent lived there, getting by as they raised rye and maintained a large vegetable garden. Johanna was what the Germans call a "pearl," and we became good friends. So the idea grew that I should be sent to the Hantels' farm for a couple of months in the summer to live the healthy life. One element in that life was to eat what the others were eating, and I dutifully did my best with the simple, hearty food we were served, rejecting only the blood sausage.

Certainly my appetite improved in this unaccustomed setting; I came to love this life and my new "parents," who became "Vati" and "Mutti" to me. Showing their trust in me, they assigned me to important chores like feeding the chickens. Almost every day I would go to the fields with my new companions to watch them at work. Duly warned that the scythes they used were extremely sharp, I learned to stay away from them, just as after a few days I got used to the stinking outhouse. My most triumphant moment of the season came when the Hantels brought in the harvest and I could sit atop a wagon heavily loaded with bundled rye, swaying as it pulled from the fields to the barn. In Kümmritz I even learned to discount the threat of thunderstorms, for I witnessed some devastating ones without suffering, and eventually without fearing, the lightning that struck all around me.

But during the school year, it was up to my parents to be inventive about my deplorable eating habits. I did not discover this until long after my childhood was over, but these parents, with whom I imagined myself a full-fledged partner in Fröhlich and Co., were not altogether innocent of well-intentioned fraud. One part of their program for me was no secret, to feed me large quantities of my favorite food: chocolate bars, chocolate candy, chocolate pudding, to say nothing of my daily Mohrenkopf. Not even I could find fault with this menu. But they also devised a plan to trick me into eating a more nutritious diet. One day—I must have been six—my parents took me to a variety theatre. Berlin was famous for these entertainment palaces, and one of these, the Scala, seemed exceptionally attractive to me, for it featured famous clowns, comedians, dancers, bands, vocalists doing favorite numbers from popular operettas. At the Scala I saw Grock, the great clown, desperately trying and always failing to construct a human bridge with the dubious help of a confederate. Their ever-repeated announcement that they were about to perform this feat—"Eine Brücke! Eine Brücke!"—still sounds in my ears. At the Scala, too, I saw Rastelli, the world's most remarkable juggler, performing virtual miracles such as balancing three soccer balls, one on top of the other, on one foot.

Now, on this first occasion, my father alerted me that before we would be admitted to the Scala, a tall fellow in a colorful uniform guarding the entrance would ask me if I always finished my dinner. My father was my authority for just about everything, but I refused to swallow this. Yet sure enough, as we got to the entrance of the Scala, a gorgeously attired doorman, complete with glacé gloves, ornate coat with golden buttons, and fanciful headgear, did ask me about my dinners. My father confessed many years later that he had bribed the man for my own good. Thus he kept his paternal authority intact, and my eating improved—for a time. But by 1933 we had greater worries. We had suddenly become Jews.

THREE

The Opium of the Masses

There are three ways of becoming a Jew: by birth, by conversion, by decree. Brushed by only a breath of the first, I was forcibly enlisted in the third group after January 30, 1933. Many years later, after settling in the United States, I was accused more than once of not being "Jewish enough." In 1943, when I was a freshman at the University of Denver, I joined an informal discussion group of Methodist students led by Harvey Potthoff, a minister who after more than fifty-five years is still my friend. This "desertion" displeased one Robert Gamzey, who had heard of the circle and denounced me in his regular column in the insignificant weekly he edited, the *Rocky Mountain Jewish News:* I of all people, a refugee from Hitler, should have stuck with my own kind! The Nazis had no such problem with me.

My parents made me into a village atheist, and, with a few psychological refinements, I have remained one. No adolescent struggles with the faith of my fathers for me—I had no faith to lose and was perfectly comfortable with a condition that more devout people have described as sadly deprived. My parents were so sure of their disbelief in God and their disdain for rituals and practices that agnosticism struck them as a tepid compromise. In fact, my father was convinced that Jesus was not a historical figure but a priestly invention.

The idea of attachment to a social community or a common heritage, then, was virtually meaningless to my parents. Jewish awareness? Jewish identity? These were empty slogans to them—and hence to me. All that was for theologians. The thought that Judaism could be anything more than a religion entered their minds only glancingly. They might playfully admit that there was something "typically Jewish" about the modernity of which Berlin was the undisputed headquarters. When, in 1928, the Ullstein house brought out a new tabloid called *Tempo*, designed with its pungent headlines, spirited editing, and ample illustrations to catch the attention of the Berliner who read as he ran, the paper was quickly dubbed "Die jüdische Hast," perhaps best translated as "Jewish nervousness." When as an adolescent I declared that if I were ever to get married, it would be to a gentile, I was only pushing to its limits my parents' uncompromising rejection of any tribal identification. Of course, we had Jewish friends and relatives more Jewish than we were. But my father found his closest friends in business and in sports, and his professional associates and the soccer players and sprinters he knew and liked were nearly all gentiles. And without the help of some of them, we would probably have ended up in the gas chambers.

There was a moment in the early 1950s—I am not proud of this memory—when, puffed up with anthropological wisdom recently acquired at Columbia, I lectured my father on the vulgarity of atheism and the need to understand the social function of religion; already in poor health, amazed at my defection, and unequal to any serious discussion, he went to bed weeping. I was appalled at what I had done and welcomed my mother's suggestion that I apologize the next morning. I did so gladly, and all was well again. I did not repeat that lapse. I was in the process of discovering Freud in those years, and he promptly restored my unbeliever's equilibrium by his teaching and his example.

I bring no news when I reveal that people are not consistent. My parents did not altogether abandon all ties to Jewishness, however little it meant to them. They liked to salt their talk with a few Yiddish words—*ganif, meschugge, risches,* and the like—words that were beginning to enter general German usage. But they were particularly allergic to *goy,* the derisive term many Jews apply to gentiles. They did not explicitly warn me against this epithet, but I must have learned to share their aversion: I still cringe when I hear it today. At the same time—and this is the inconsistency I have in mind—they freely used the abbreviation "g.n.," which stands for *goyim naches,* a gentile's pleasure, to describe such foolhardy activities as mountain climbing or water skiing. But the implication that Jews are too smart to engage voluntarily in such suicidal adventures was all too thin a reed on which to hang one's Jewish identity.

They had me circumcised. Why? Was it a remainder of Jewish identification or a medical procedure? Why did my father light a candle on the anniversaries of his parents' deaths? A touch of surviving Jewish loyalties or an expression of private, secular piety? I do not know; we never talked about it. But in any event, these gestures did not define my parents. They were Germans. True, my father did put his name in an address book of Jewish merchants in Berlin in the late 1920s. But that was business.

My upbringing was not simply irreligious; it was antireligious. My father, bluff and outspoken, left no doubt where he stood in the historic battle between reason and unreason. With his bellicose view of past and present, he was a true son of the Enlightenment. My mother, less emphatic than my father, needed no pressure or persuasion to be, like her husband, wholly secular. The first time I heard the name of Karl Marx was when my father spoke to me about a brilliant thinker who had lived a hundred years before me and who had said, wisely, that religion is the opium of the masses. In a reminiscent mood, my father told me that he had turned atheist when he was twelve, and he boasted that his step-mother (his father, Salo Fröhlich, had married twice) had specified in her will that no rabbi be allowed to preside at her funeral. In January 1955, when he died, my father took the same route: he asked that no religious ceremony be performed, but that someone say a few words. My friend Harvey Potthoff, the Methodist minister he had come to know, performed that duty. If my father could not abide Christianity, he had no objections to individual Christians.

The malicious anecdote or the debunking of biblical passages, favorite gambits that had served unbelievers for centuries, were prominent features in my religious upbringing. How did Moses manage to write the Pentateuch after his death? How did Jesus (assuming that he had existed at all) rise to heaven two days after his execution? Exploring his own experience, my father liked to tell me about a devout Jew in Kempen who consulted his rabbi concerning a chicken he had just bought. Was it kosher even though it had a kernel of grain stuck in its gullet? The rabbi, only too aware of the petitioner's poverty, let the fowl pass. A more tolerant and less determined campaigner might have used this episode as evidence that some men of God at least had good sense and put life above ritual. But my father saw it as just one more proof of the incurable hypocrisy and unmitigated absurdity of all religion.

The triumphs of form over substance and greed over reverence were my father's abiding themes when sacred matters came up. In spite of all protestations, he said, religion, every religion, failed to make people less cruel or more moral. Quite the contrary, it provided alibis for egotism, bigotry, hypocrisy, and the release of aggressive impulses. The Jews of Kempen, to whom my father returned repeatedly for his examples, served his didactic purposes well. Aware that their creed forbade them to handle money on the Sabbath but unwilling to forgo the income that a store open on Saturdays brought, they would shove their takings into the cash register with their elbows. It did not occur to me then that this was a tale as improbable as it was tendentious: these stories quite suited me. By 1959, when I published a book on that great scoffer Voltaire, my father was dead. But I know that this work would have pleased him very much.

To underscore their distance from all religiosity, my parents officially left the Jewish community and declared themselves, and me, *konfessionslos*—without denomination. This is what I would tell my teacher in elementary school when, in the first class meeting of each year, he took our vital statistics. Their declaration had tax consequences. The *konfessionslosen* in Weimar Germany did not pay less, but none of their contributions to the state treasury went to support churches or synagogues. (Of course, not all who officially declared themselves free of ties to any denomination were Jews: gentile Social Democrats publicly cut what their Marxist doctrine told them were leading strings that curbed their freedom of action and insulted their dignity as rational beings.) Thus liberated, my parents did not scruple to put up a Christmas tree and hide Easter eggs. To their mind, both of these holidays were simply secular; their Christian trappings struck them as superficial decor. For all this, they had no intention of concealing their origins, as many Jews had done, by converting to Christianity. Baptism might bring social and professional dividends, but for my parents such an act would have meant exchanging one superstition for another. As it turned out, of course, the Nazis' racial definition of Jewishness would have made any such subterfuge irrelevant.

Piety could hardly grow on so barren a soil, although, as I have suggested, I did not regret my godless condition. I thought, a little melodramatically, that it made me a free man. But my parents' resolute refusal to make Jewishness an essential quality in our lives generated conflicts in our immediate family. Tante Hede, the woman who was unfortunately always right, managed the religious practices, such as they were, of her husband and sons, their extent and their limits. They amounted to very little: in our house we derisively called her a *drei-Tage Jude,* a "three-day Jew," the widespread designation for German Jews who mixed ignorance with occasional, somewhat shamefaced, demonstrations of religious allegiance. For three days a year—the first and second day of Rosh Hashana and on Yom Kippur—they would buy tickets for religious services and then forget about observance for another year.

Not content with dictating three-day Jewishness to her own family, Tante Hede tried to impose this limited commitment on my parents, and of necessity on me. She had reckoned without my father. He let her know that such matters were entirely our business. This strong stance was not mere family pride or a way of protecting my mother from being bullied but also a matter of principle. He firmly believed, and told me more than once, that civilized people avoid intruding on the way others raise their children.

Although she could not boss my parents or me, Tante Hede made me uncomfortable in another way: she elected me as a model that my cousin Edgar would do well to imitate. Her firstborn, Hanns, needed no model. With a partiality that made me wince, Tante Hede preferred Hanns, three years older than I, to Edgar, three months my junior. Hanns could do no wrong, Edgar no right. That this treatment was unjust and counterproductive was obvious to me even then, and obvious to everyone else except Tante Hede. It was almost predictable that Edgar, a decent, lovable, and unloved boy who was a stranger to open resentment, should more or less eat himself to death in his fifties. A little naive at times, given to indiscretions and to jokes that few appreciated, Edgar did less well in school than his native intelligence would have warranted. All this made me, the good pupil and the good boy, a living reproach to him.

In spite of all her authority, though, Tante Hede failed to

reshape not just my parents' religious attitudes but even those of her sons. One memorable episode brought it all out. I was a fanatical fan of Berlin's best soccer team, Hertha B.S.C., which Hanns also supported. In his usual role of odd boy out, Edgar rooted for Hertha's only interesting local rival, Tennis Borussia, a stand that produced some enjoyable verbal tussles among us. As soon as I could use the buses and subways on my own, my parents permitted me to attend important Hertha games alone. Since I could easily prove that each game my team played at home was important, I was at the Hertha stadium every other Sunday. One year, I think it was 1935, a high holiday fell on a Sunday, and Hertha was playing at home—naturally an important match. For my parents this was a nonissue: of course I would watch the game.

My cousins, though, were not so fortunate; the tickets for temple services had been bought, and Hanns and Edgar were expected to attend without fail. But if there was one thing they craved, it was to join me. Together, we worked out an infallible scheme: they would go to the temple, have their tickets stamped, exclaim with mimed horror that they had forgotten their prayer books, and rush off to the stadium. I don't know who won, even who Hertha's opponent was, but I recall the unpleasant denouement. Edgar could not contain himself and leaked the escapade at home that evening. Luckily I was not present to witness the scene, but I can visualize the rhetorical storms, the meaningless threats, and Tante Hede's certainty that Edgar was the villain in the piece.

A second episode, rather more serious, will convey the kind of rationality we cultivated at home. Early in 1934, for the sake of giving me some company and some much needed exercise—I was fairly clumsy and unathletic—my parents enrolled me in what was in effect a Jewish boy scout troop. It was called the Ringbund, its emblem a ring inscribed on a pennant. It was an echo, I found out many years later, of the symbol that Jews in the Middle Ages were compelled to wear as a sign of identification. Under normal circumstances, my parents would not have chosen the Ringbund for me, but circumstances were not normal. We wore gray shirts and gray neckerchiefs edged in black and looked for all the world like serious outdoors types, though emphatically different from the Hitler Youth, with their swaggering, militarist bearing. We of the Ringbund went on hikes, at times on overnight excursions. I must record that the tents we put up had a tendency to collapse over our heads.

Then in 1935, when I was twelve, the leader of the troop attempted to persuade me to have a bar mitzvah. My cousin Hanns had undergone such a ceremony, though for reasons now obscure to me I had not attended it. The idea did not intrigue me; my parents and I had never canvassed such a step. I was troubled by the prospect of saying prayers that I did not understand or believe in, and of becoming a man in so superstitious an ambience. I pleaded ignorance, indifference, even hostility: the Jewish religion meant nothing to me. Shrewdly, the scout leader, who must have been all of eighteen, countered with a secular argument: these were hard times for Jews. In two years of power, the Nazis had done their utmost to defame us, to drive us out of public life and, if they could, out of the country. I needed to declare my solidarity with a persecuted people; to join the Jewish community through a bar mitzvah would be an act of goodwill so necessary these days.

To my astonishment, I found his arguments persuasive and came home to ask my parents to let me prepare for a bar mitzvah. I rather bewildered them, but they soon recovered, falling quite naturally into the liberal, rationalist pattern of thinking that had, they believed—and I believed—served us three so well before. They did not voice alarm; rather, they told me that if a bar mitzvah was what I really wanted, they would support my having one. But if I only wanted extra presents, they would see to it that my thirteenth birthday produced an exceptionally rich haul.

Here was another instance of my parents' treating me as

an adult. Would it not have been better to take the burden of decision from my shoulders and to wax indignant—"no child of mine will go through this routine"? Their way of handling this matter did not surprise me in the least and at the time greatly pleased me. My second thoughts emerged only later. At the time, though, I thought and thought, and the atheist won out. No bar mitzvah for me but, as promised, extra presents, some valuable stamps, some longed-for books. Thinking back now on my petty internal drama in the light of the threats gathering about us, it seems trivial, almost silly. But it remains worth underscoring that, caught in the maelstrom of historic upheavals, we German Jews had to live our ordinary lives, struggling for grades at school, going to the dentist, buying groceries for dinner, visiting friends, in addition to worrying about the Nazis' plans for us and about the precise contours of our Jewishness. And on that last point, we three, apart from the momentary deviation I have described, did not waver. At a time when more and more Jewish families were placing their children in Jewish schools away from anti-Semitic slights, my parents had no such plans for me, and I never pressed them. Did we not have some fairly persuasive indications—I am speaking of the first years of Nazi rule—that the future might not be quite so gloomy as some Cassandras were predicting?

Mixed Signals

Nature and my parents seem to have prepared me well for the hazards of daily life under the Nazis. I had blue eyes and a straight nose, brown hair and regular features—in short, like my parents, I did not "look Jewish." I had a peculiar obsession in those days: when I saw myself in the mirror, I judged my appearance to be just as it should be, while others, like my somewhat pudgy cousin Edgar, with his curly hair, fell off from the standard I set—a case of boyish narcissism, perhaps (I am ashamed even to think this) fed by the official propaganda touting the Teutonic looks that were, according to Nazi ideology, the ideal. I, too, looked as German as any. And my upbringing seemed almost intentionally aimed at having me escape particular notice, whether on the street, in a department store, or at a soccer stadium. I was composed and polite, and did not invite attention.

On a deeper level, too, I was ready, though of course I was quite ignorant of this at the time. Having learned to banish from awareness, or at least to control, my rage, I was not about to make uncalled-for remarks or even faces at fluttering black-red-and-white flags adorned with the swastika or the sordid spectacle of brownshirts marching down Berlin's streets as though they owned them—as, of course, they did after January 30, 1933. I was exposed to such exhibitions nearly every day: the Nazis were adroit at political theatre. They even uprooted the venerable linden trees lining the city's most distinguished avenue, Unter den Linden, to make more room for displays of flags and uniformed marchers. I had been well trained to show no reaction, make no comment. Not that I was trying to pass; I was born to pass.

The advent of the Third Reich is a blank in my mind—a conspicuous instance of repression at work. After all, my parents and my wider family must have talked about the Nazis' bid for power every day, and anxiously; certainly the press was full of it. But my first firm memory of that period dates from February 28, four weeks after Hitler's appointment as chancellor: a large photo showing smoke billowing over the roof of the Reichstag. That vast pile, dating from the late nineteenth century, had been set on fire the day before. A young, not very bright Dutch Communist named Marinus van der Lubbe was quickly arrested and confessed to having committed the arson on his own.

The story was unbelievable. Years later, when I was working on the history of the Weimar Republic and its pathetic end, I read in the much-quoted diary of Harry Graf Kessler, aesthete, patron of the arts, and principled anti-Nazi: "This ca. twenty-year-old is supposed to have distributed inflammable material in more than thirty places and set them alight without anyone's noticing his presence or activity or his carting in all these massive amounts of material." Kessler did not believe the story put out by the controlled press, nor did my parents: surely Göring had set the fire for political reasons, to supply his fellow gangsters with a convenient excuse for terrorizing whatever opposition remained. They talked knowingly about a secret tunnel leading to the Reichstag basement, through which the arsonists had carried the supplies they needed to start this convenient conflagration.

With characteristic dispatch and raw efficiency, the Nazis tightened their grip on power, mixing cajolery with lies, threats, and violence. The Reichstag fire provided them with apparently good reasons for pushing through an emergency decree, beating up journalists, politicians, and ordinary citizens known to be insufficiently supportive, arresting opposition leaders, forcing intellectuals into exile, and mobilizing public opinion with a propaganda machine of unprecedented intensity. In light of this politics of brutality and seduction and the laming of all independent opinion, the elections to the Reichstag of March 5 were scarcely the triumph that the regime's spokesmen proclaimed them to be: the Nazis secured just under 44 percent of the vote. Had it been a free election, that figure would have been significantly lower. But this did not stop them; on March 23, the Reichstag voted an enabling act that essentially handed its powers to the Hitlerian regime.

It was not to be expected that Germany's new masters would overlook the Jews. On April 1 they staged a countrywide boycott of Jewish stores, lawyers, and physicians. Brownshirts and black-shirted s.s. men, posted at strategic spots, "warned" potential customers and clients against patronizing Jews—not Germans. Enormous posters plastered on walls and kiosks proclaimed, "The Jews of the whole world want to destroy Germany! German Volk! Defend yourself! Do not buy from Jews!" Certainly in Berlin this "action" was not much of a success. But what bodily threats and inflammatory slogans did not accomplish, servile institutions managed with ease.

Professional organizations hastened to expel "non-Aryan" writers and newspapermen, while orchestras and theatres dismissed conductors, directors, and performers they judged to be racially ineligible or politically tainted. The Jewish professors' turn came soon after, while Jewish executives in banks, commerce, and industry were prematurely pensioned. On April 7 a comprehensive Civil Service Act excluded Jews from all public employment. The exodus was well under way. For the fortunate few, like Franz Neumann, the decision to flee to freedom was forced on them. For less well-prepared men like my father, with no foreign languages or other portable specialty, the situation was less clear-cut and the prospects exceedingly obscure. They were complicated further by the mixed signals that were all we had to go on.

My admission to gymnasium and my years there were one long demonstration of these signals at work. In the spring of 1933 the larger new world and my own small corner of it intersected. I had successfully completed four years of elementary education, and unlike working-class boys, who would continue in their free school for four more years, I, with other young bourgeois, was destined for more elevated secondary schooling, costing my parents twenty marks a month. There were distinct types of gymnasia in the Germany of my childhood, ranging from the classical version, which had retained Greek in its curriculum, to more modern real-gymnasia, oriented toward nonacademic careers. The Goethe-Real-Schule for which I was headed was of the second type: it started ten-year-olds with French and after two years offered a choice between two tracks, one starting Latin and the other English. Though relatively progressive, it was traditional enough to call its classes by Latin numerals, some of them oddly yoked to German prefixes: Sexta, Quinta, Quarta, Unter-Tertia, Ober-Tertia, and the rest.

During the Weimar Republic, my admission to a gymnasium would have been a matter of course; my parents' class and my grades would have guaranteed it. Now, though, a newly proclaimed policy restricted the numbers of Jewish boys to be accepted. Their percentage was not to exceed the percentage of Jews in Berlin's population—more than 150,000 in four million, just under 4 percent. But a special circumstance exempted me from any quota: my father had been wounded in the First World War, a condition much honored in Germany and one that conferred a certain status on the veteran. In 1915 he had been shot in the right hand and the right upper arm; the scars, pale little rosettes, were still visible. The wounds kept my father from stretching out his arm to full length, though this hardly handicapped him: in the mid-1930s he became a champion bowler. Still, this relatively minor disability was enough to make him the recipient of the Iron Cross Second Class and entitled him to privileges like riding first class on a second-class railroad ticket and receiving a monthly pension. And now, in March 1933, it gave his son an unquestioned place in a gymnasium of his choice.

My father, like most Germans, had greeted the coming of the war in early August 1914 with patriotic enthusiasm, but he soon turned pacifist. I once asked him when he had switched camps. "In September 1914," he told me, "when I saw my first corpse." I should add that he threw his pacifist ideals overboard in September 1939, the moment Britain and France declared war against the Axis. Later, after Pearl Harbor, nothing pleased him more than to contribute his German medal to the scrap drive collecting metal for the American war effort. For this gesture his picture appeared in the Denver papers.

For three years, until 1936, when we moved some fifteen minutes farther away, I had a five-minute walk from Schweid-nitzerstrasse 5 to the big, solid, airy building that was supposed to be my school for the next nine years. I have a photograph of a class excursion in my third year, with twenty-one students surrounding our Latin teacher, Dr. Rose, bald, bespectacled, corpulent, wearing an old-fashioned suit complete with vest, stand-up collar, and narrow tie. Rose represented the best my gymnasium had to offer me: a teacher of the old school who was neither a martinet nor an anti-Semite. He had grown old with the Goethe-Real-Schule, having taught there since its opening in 1907, and he brought a whiff of the more decent aspects of the Wilhelminian Empire into the postwar and even into the Nazi world.

I recognize my cousin Edgar in that photo, smiling, and at least one other Jewish pupil, named Landsberg, who, I recall, was not the brightest. Two other classmates stand out:

Rutkowsky, who looks like a working-class bully (though he never bullied me), with a square face and a pugilist's flat nose, and, standing with his arm on my shoulder in a comradely gesture, the ash-blond Hans Schmidt. This shows how photographs lie. May his bones lie rotting in Russian soil!

There was something truly repulsive about Hans Schmidt, and that is why he deserves his fifteen seconds of fame here. He was as unathletic as I and more cowardly. The compulsory workouts at the gym were torture to me; I could never leap over the leather-covered wooden horse without a sense of panic, and Hans Schmidt, I like to believe, felt the same way. But while my timidity hurt no one else, Hans Schmidt was more malicious; he aimed to wound without taking responsibility. Whatever anti-Semitic talk there was among my classmates was largely at his instigation, and he incited others to do the dirty work for him, though, if memory serves, often without success.

I remember running into him in my first year at the gymnasium as I was walking with my parents on the Paulsbornerstrasse, which linked us to the other Fröhlich family on the Pariserstrasse; he stopped to talk to us, courteous and respectful. But once he joined the Hitler Jugend, as he quickly did, he sported his uniform and became a little Nazi who had no use for me. In class he had no rivals—I saw to that. He was consistently the best student, the Primus, though I was convinced that I was brighter than he; I simply held back out of prudence, managing to stay in second place. I do not think that I ever explicitly formulated this policy; this act of self-protection had become second nature to me.

The pressure on Jewish pupils at the Goethe Gymnasium was selective: I was never ridiculed, never harassed, never attacked, not even slyly, to the best of my recollection. My cousin Edgar, in contrast, was victimized more than once, threatened with being dragged before a *Stürmer* display and made to read it. The *Stürmer*—need I remind anyone?—was the pornographic anti-Semitic weekly edited by Julius Streicher, which featured stories and cartoons depicting savagely caricatured Jews, with repellent curly hair, grotesquely hooked noses, evil eyes, and fat, sensual lips, busy cheating the world, orchestrating hostility to the Third Reich, and, worse, lusting after blonde, often half-naked Aryan women. I do not believe that Edgar was ever put through this trial, but he had every right to be uncomfortable at his school. I find it soothing to recall that Streicher was convicted at the Nürnberg trials and hanged—he is a principal reason that my opposition to the death penalty has always been half-hearted.

For an institution under the Nazis, my school had a remarkably bland, almost unpolitical atmosphere. Its authoritarianism, such as it was, seemed less an obeisance to Hitlerite Germany than a legacy from earlier times. We sat in orderly rows, each of us at an assigned desk that was nailed to the floor, as was the chair. We knew our place and were quite literally unmovable, a situation one might read as a symbol of stability or, doubtless more accurately, of rigidity. The desks themselves were uniform, with a slanting top that could be lifted to reveal a storage space for books and papers. When a teacher entered the room, we rose to our feet, a sign of respect we did not always feel. And those of us called on to recite in class wormed our way out of our tight quarters to move forward, standing just below the teacher, whose table rested on a raised platform.

The prevailing tone in my school was sober, even though our teachers did not terrorize us. But the exuberance with which we welcomed moments of levity suggests that we felt under considerable pressure most of the time. I remember one day when a young substitute teacher took our class; clearly nervous about his assignment, he was a heaven-sent victim. Sensing his vulnerability, with the cruelty of youth at full flood, we went wild, yelling with abandon, throwing water-soaked sponges, exploiting a rare and thus all the more valued opportunity to let go. To the best of my memory, no

Jewish pupil was ever handled at the Goethe Gymnasium as pitilessly as this apprentice.

Another moment of levity remains with me, trifling no doubt but telling for the atmosphere I am trying to recapture: once in our fourth year—that is, in the Unter-Tertia—a pupil kept raising his hand and asking permission to go to the bathroom. When the teacher objected that he had already done so not long before, the student replied succinctly: *"Sextaner-blase."* He was regretting—or boasting?—that he had the bladder of a first-year pupil. This laconic one-word reply, a good instance of Berlin humor in action, struck us all as terribly funny—evidence that humor was rarely on our menu.

This calm climate proved a blessing to the Jewish pupils at the school. If we were singled out at all, it was during the historic festivities when the students were called together to the auditorium—the *Aula*—to imbibe a broadcast speech by the Führer. In 1935 the Saarland, which by the peace treaties following the First World War had been placed under the auspices of the League of Nations, voted to return to the fatherland. We Jewish students were not permitted to join our schoolmates in the celebration that followed. Nor were we ever forced to sing the Horst-Wessel Lied or other Nazi hymns. Many years later, an American interviewer, furious with my parents for failing to transfer me to a Jewish school, wondered how I must have felt when I had to sing that awful verse about Jewish blood spurting from a knife—*wenn jü-disch' Blut vom Messer spritzt.* I could only tell her that during my years at the Goethe Gymnasium, I had never even heard that song, let alone been compelled to join in. Our teachers were on the whole free of bigotry and did not set out to make their Jewish pupils' lives harder than those of our gentile classmates.

Among the anti-Semitic minority, a history teacher known for his sarcasm occasionally made cutting remarks about Jews but kept away from grosser displays. At least once, I think, he must have realized that his doctrinal sallies made for bad history in his pupils' already confused minds: our assignment for the week was the Reformation, and he asked one of the two or three Catholics in the class, from a poorer background than the rest of us and rather stupid, "Who was it that gave the papacy so much trouble in the sixteenth century?" The boy fished around for an answer, could not come up with Martin Luther, and hazarded a counterquestion: "the Jews?" We all broke down and roared, including the teacher, who was of course responsible for the mischief in the first place.

A second teacher, as far as I can recall, lost control just once. He was supposedly teaching us French, though he did very little beyond loading us down with a swarm of isolated irregular verbs and linguistic subtleties. He had asked Landsberg to translate a passage in which the word *pluie* occurred, and Landsberg rendered it *Wolkenbruch*—cloudburst. This is admittedly rather strong for *rain,* but I was baffled when our teacher responded with a cloudburst of his own: "The Jews always exaggerate!" he shouted. This was news to me, and I found the accusation troubling. Was hyperbole one of those Jewish defects that the Nazi authorities kept denouncing? Or was this just another instance of the lies my father had warned me about? Perhaps loading down a casual explosion with heavy significance, I have sometimes wondered whether my unremitting search for precision in my writing was in part fueled by this outburst. I had, and have, no answer, but that "cloudburst" has stayed with me.

The question remains: was my gymnasium at all typical of schools during the Third Reich? Other memoirs throw doubt on it. To quote but one instance from Ernest G. Heppner, who attended a gymnasium in Breslau and survived by emigrating to Shanghai: "The beginning of the isolation of the Jewish population hit schoolchildren the hardest. Every school day the anti-Semitic pressure became more noticeable as teachers joined pupils in verbal and, in some cases, physical attacks on Jewish children. Nazi propaganda was introduced into every facet of the teaching material and curriculum. Especially obnoxious to me were the teachings about the 'science' of race, and the continuous references to 'foreign elements' and racially inferior pupils" (*Shanghai Refuge: A Memoir of the World War II Jewish Ghetto* [1993], 12). And yet I can report only on my own past, even if—especially if—it contradicts widespread clichés about Germans. My years in the Goethe Gymnasium attested to surviving pockets of decency in Nazi Germany, even of quiet resistance. And this further complicated our assessment of what we had to expect.

I am not, of course, suggesting that the Goethe Gymnasium was totally free of the Nazi taint—how could it have been? And I can testify from experience to an anti-Semitic lie that had its counterpart across the country and has become a familiar part of refugee lore. It reads almost like an archetypal fiction illustrating the comprehensiveness of Nazi mendacity and inhumanity, but it is true enough. Twice a week we had music, which consisted mainly of singing songs. I can still visualize a page of our songbook opened to the "Lorelei," a famous art song after a poem by Heinrich Heine. But our textbook, obviously revised after January 1933, listed its author as "unknown." In the Third Reich, Heine had become a nonperson. A hundred years before Hitler, Heine had observed that a country that burns books will one day burn people. He could not have known that his dire, apparently extravagant prediction would come true one day. How many of us in the mid-1930s, Nazis included, had any inkling that Germany's Jews would become nonpersons in more fatal ways?

Not all of life, to be sure, was school. I filled much time with extracurricular activities: radio broadcasts of automobile races or track and field meets were frequent, welcome interruptions of my routine as a pupil. Around this time, too, I discovered Berlin's great museums. The Pergamon Museum, with its impressive reconstructions of a grandiose Roman temple and of a street in ancient Babylon, was a particular favorite. In my own boyish, not particularly well-informed way, I also adopted certain paintings, mainly from the Dutch seventeenth century. There, too, I formed distinct attachments, above all Rembrandt's *Man in a Golden Helmet*. Surely, I told myself, this depiction of a brooding, strong old man wearing a brilliantly rendered helmet must be the most magnificent painting ever painted! That many years later this gem was demoted as not being a Rembrandt at all has not lessened my affection for it.

Then—need I say it?—there was reading, and reading some more. Some time around 1934 I had stumbled on Berlin's *bouquinistes*, outdoor booksellers who offered their wares from large open carts. Each of the titles I fancied was precisely two or three signatures long—that is, sixty-four or ninety-six pages. The best thing about this open-air booksellers' trade was that you could return your purchase and, for a small payment, acquire another detective story, another novel of adventure. I had been getting an allowance since I was five, and though I also spent money on birthday presents for my parents, I used most of it on this literature.

The plots of the cheap paperbacks I regularly selected escape me now, but they must have been tailored to a single formula. I remember that I doted on an interminable series of crime stories featuring a detective called John Kling—of course an American. This suited my yearnings in these years; the United States was much on my mind. As I have noted before, more than once during my childhood, my American relatives—Onkel Alfred, Aunt Grace, and their only child, Albert, known as Aboo—came to Berlin to visit my maternal grandmother, and their presence only enlivened my fantasies of spending my life in their country, for a far better future than I could expect in Germany.

Not all the books I bought or borrowed were quite so inexpensive as the John Kling mysteries. I have already mentioned the magical name of the prolific adventure writer Karl

May, a taste for whose books—he wrote well more than sixty of them—I shared with untold thousands of German boys. May had an adventurous story of his own. Born to a destitute family in Saxony, he grew up to be a thief and confidence artist, invariably caught and punished. It was in prison that he discovered his "literary" gift, and by the 1890s, he had made himself into a national celebrity with a series of tales. In all of them he was the thinly disguised hero: an unerring shot, an unrivaled rider, an unbeatable wrestler, a loyal friend, a Christian gentleman. May was an outstanding exemplar of the professional liar. The theatres in which his banal but suspenseful novels played out included lands of the imagination, the Near East and, providentially for me, the United States. His best-loved invention was a trilogy, *Winnetou,* in which the German hero, not surprisingly called Charlie and also known as Old Shatterhand, becomes the intimate of an Apache chief and almost marries the chief's sister. I need hardly add that these reading orgies did not exclude more serious fare. By the time I was twelve I boasted, largely thanks to my parents, a small library of a dozen books or more, housed in the buffet, several of them the amusingly illustrated histories and geographies by the Dutch popularizer Willem van Loon.

I liked writing as much as reading; at school and at home, I found putting words together one of my chief satisfactions— at times a flight from feelings of despair, more often a sheer delight. In my later years, after I had become an academic, colleagues at times professed themselves awed by my literary productivity, or openly envious of it. Anyone who had seen me scribbling when I was twelve or fourteen would not have been astonished. But I regret to say that my early contributions to modern fiction and drama are lost; like much else that belonged to us, we did not rescue them into freedom. The plot of the comedy I wrote and its every detail have sunk into the black hole of the irrecoverably forgotten. I do remember that it was an imitation of the sophisticated one-acters by the contemporary German playwright Walter Goetz, now almost unknown, long on wit and short on action. The novel I perpetrated, though, remains fairly clear in my mind. I managed to fill six sturdy exercise books, inventing a world war between the forces of good and evil. Some of the conflict played out on the moon, and the outcome depended, I recall, on which side could develop the better spacecraft; it was of course the good guys who succeeded. I was my own Jules Verne.

Nor did I neglect the occasional get-togethers of the Ringbund. One day, however, we were brushed by history. It was a Sunday morning, July 1, 1934, and our troop was to meet at an elevated station in the far northwest corner of Berlin to go on a hike. As we drifted in one after another, our troop leader hastily told us to take off our neckerchiefs, hide them in our pockets, and go home as quietly as we could. There was trouble. When I reached home, I learned that Hitler had ordered a bloodbath among old followers and imagined rivals, some of them his lieutenants for years. The most spectacular victim of the purge was Ernst Röhm, head of the brown-shirted S.A., who, with other longtime political allies, was shot to death that day or the next.

The total number of casualties has never been firmly established, but it cannot have been fewer than 150, at least twice the official figure. The justification offered to the controlled press, which obediently published it under screaming headlines, was the homosexual conduct of Röhm and several others; a few had been found in bed with what were called *Lustknaben*, perhaps best rendered as "joy boys." What was more, we were told, all of them had plotted treason. My parents' excitement was palpable. Perhaps one blood-soaked civil war among the Nazi leadership might generate another—one of those vain hopes with which we beguiled our anxious days. But the story greatly puzzled me. I could understand (if not believe) the charge that these men had joined forces to overthrow their leader. But what was homosexuality? What

precisely was a Lustknabe? My parents were not very informative; plainly, their liberalism stopped short at throwing light
on the wilder shores of sexuality for me.

During the early months of the following year, the time
for a consequential decision was upon us. Which track was
I to select in the Goethe Schule once I had been promoted
to the third class, the quarta: Latin or English? To my parents
and to me, the choice was clear. We did not yet speak much
of emigration, but we expected that sooner or later we would
move to the United States. Hence we had no difficulty: it
would be English. But then my father got a telephone call
from *Oberstudiendirektor* Dr. Quandt, the head of the Goethe-
Real-Schule: would my father come and see him? We could
not imagine why. I could not recall any moral or scholarly
dereliction on my part—was Dr. Quandt going to nudge me
more or less tactfully from my gymnasium? Not at all. Quandt
told my father that he disagreed with our decision to have
me take the modern option. I was beyond question a talented
pupil, he said, and therefore belonged in the traditional Latin
class. Overpowered by this flattery, my father consented. The
conversation made a considerable impression on my family.
Talk about mixed signals!

Were we naive to listen to Quandt? Our stake in my education was greater than his. Quandt could hardly be a good
Nazi; was he, then, a pliant time server? In March 1936 and
1937, our local newspaper, *Der Westen,* reported our school's
annual graduation ceremonies—I was still there but excused
from such rites—over which Quandt presided. In a manner
that the most rabid party member would have applauded, he
singled out the best students of the year, presented them with
ornately bound copies of Hitler's *Mein Kampf* and Alfred Rosenberg's muddled, highly influential racist tract, *The Myth
of the Twentieth Century.* Then, in the name of the school,
he swore fidelity to the Führer. Germany's two national an-
thems, "Deutschland, Deutschland über alles" and the Horst-

Wessel Lied, closed the festivities. This was the man who had not long before taken the trouble to persuade my father that a youngster of my abilities should not bother with English.

Mixed signals! In the year I started Latin in my school, Onkel Siegfried—my mother's, not my father's, brother—was awarded the *Ehren-Kreuz,* the Cross of Honor, given to soldiers who had served at the front in the First World War. The document, presented by Berlin's police commissioner, was issued in the name of "the Führer and Chancellor." It now looks like a joke or a forgery, but it is authentic. I hold the piece of paper in my hand and do not know whether to laugh or to throw up. I look again: the signature is unmistakably a facsimile of Berlin's police chief, and he speaks, just as unmistakably, in Hitler's name. Yet only three years later, the patriot so honored became the despised stranger deprived of his livelihood, and two years after that the pariah the Führer wanted to murder. How to make sense of this screed? Incomplete coordination in Nazi officialdom? A residual uncertainty about just what to do with Germany's Jews? I think both of these conjectures are correct; it is only the testimony of the later decision for the "final solution" that makes this sign of high recognition so profoundly, so hatefully absurd.

The year 1935 also brought disappointments and dismay. It was perhaps no calamity that Onkel Max should emigrate to Palestine. He had been beaten up by Nazi hoodlums more than once, and since he was a bit of a drifter, this seemed to make a good deal of sense. He prepared himself, like other potential settlers in Palestine, by attending an agricultural training station. But my mother's situation had no remedy. In the previous year, suffering from a relatively mild case of tuberculosis, she had spent several months in a rustic sanatorium, Nordrach in the Black Forest (why do they always call the damn places "idyllic"?). In 1935, not completely cured, she had to go back for a second stay.

That was not all. Some time during these months, a letter from Johanna Hantel's father informed us that it would no longer be desirable for me to spend my summers with his family. Since Kümmritz was a hamlet where everyone knew everything about everybody, that was perhaps only to be expected. There was, as I remember it, no hostility in Hantel's tone, but the rejection hurt little less for all that. With a stroke of the pen I had lost Vati and Mutti, making it all the more important to me that I still had Papa and Mama. Then, in the fall, we had to let Johanna go. The Nürnberg Laws made her stay in our household illegal.

The history of the Nürnberg Laws has often been told. Improvised and hastily put together on the eve of the Nazi Party congress in mid-September, one of the acts deprived Jews of German citizenship, and the other, touted as protection for German blood and German honor, officially recognized the wildest racial theories and provided an alibi for harsher persecutions to come. It put severe pressures on marriages between Jews and gentiles and "interracial" extramarital affairs—the looters who raped Jewish women during the November pogrom in 1938 were punished—and it prohibited gentile women under age forty-five from working for Jews. If this statute had not been so vicious in intent and disruptive in results, we could have laughed at its childishness: as though every male Jewish employer could be expected to rape his female "Aryan" employees as long as they were sexually attractive and capable of childbearing. This provision enacted into law the lewd fantasies that the *Stürmer* was peddling weekly and cost us the services of Johanna Hantel, whom I much liked and who, I think, much liked me. Although we had good reason to believe that she went unwillingly, we never saw her again.

In contrast to the uncertainties and gloom of 1935, the year 1936 was one of memorable enjoyments. We had sweet moments of *Schadenfreude*. (Is there any significance to the fact that this word for pleasure in the discomfiture of others exists only in German?) My Onkel Siegfried, who had a wide acquaintance among his largely gentile neighbors in north Berlin, reported to us that several fanatical Nazis he knew, men with bright prospects in the party hierarchy, were disgraced when the required vigorous searches into their ancestry determined their racial heritage to be tainted. A Jewish grandfather or even a Jewish great-grandmother was enough to disqualify a German as a full Aryan. Such persons had to prove four generations of "pure blood," which is to say uncontaminated by Jewish admixtures. We now know that a number of "half-Jews" had careers in the armed services, especially if they had been raised as Christians, but these little true-life melodramas of Nazis hoist with their own petard were very welcome to us. More important: we moved to a better apartment, we went on an automobile tour through the country, and we attended the Olympics. What more could anybody ask for? And I did not go through a bar mitzvah ceremony.

Our new apartment, in the Sächsische Strasse, was larger and more comfortable than the constricted space from which we had come. My parents had a real bedroom of their own, there was a separate dining room and living room, and my quarters, though still small, were less cell-like than their predecessor. The old furniture came with us; the armoire found its proper place in my parents' bedroom, and the mighty buffet landed in the dining room. We also bought some new furniture: a modern couch with boxy loose pillows held in place by two stylish wooden bars, and a ceiling lamp fixture which sported six lightbulbs concealed in as many tinted glass saucers. It all struck me as tasteful in the extreme. We even had a little balcony—better adapted to being photographed than to sitting on, but at least we had a balcony.

These changes of fortune were yet another reminder that major public tremors and mundane private matters easily co-existed. Living under a dictatorship did not entail living consistently at a level of high tension. For Jewish lawyers without clients, Jewish actors without parts, Jewish professors without students, the persecution mania of the regime eclipsed all else. Whether to change careers, whether to emigrate, whether to seek employment in the Jewish agencies and schools the regime was foisting on us—all this mattered terribly. But for thousands of German Jews like my parents, however alert they had to be to the hostile atmosphere that bore down on them, a certain separation of spheres seemed plausible, almost appropriate. The indictment of *denial* that German Jews have had thrown at them for decades does not really fit such responses.

Our move indicated increasing affluence. Oddly enough, in the midst of Nazi chicanery, my father's business was thriving. He carried it on with a gentile partner named Kurt Pelz, a bon vivant, womanizer, and bankrupt, and with two or three traveling salesmen. The principal clients of Fröhlich and Pelz were large specialty stores and department stores, accustomed to ordering in sizable quantities. Because the firms' markup was relatively small, much depended on the ability and willingness of manufacturers to produce the goods at prices that would give their biggest customer an adequate profit. Fröhlich and Pelz existed to facilitate such arrangements.

My father's specialty was to spot a high-priced dinner service or wine glass that he thought would catch the buying public's attention in a cheaper, mass-produced version. He had a famous eye, and, quite as important, his customers trusted him, partly for his outgoing nature and partly for his principle (of which he reminded me more than once) that long-term commercial relations must rest on a foundation of honesty and candor. None of this prevented my father from playing whatever aces he had up his sleeve. In the mid-1930s he tried to win over the large retail outlet Saalberg, with a dozen branches scattered across western Germany. The company was Jewish-owned until late in the decade, and in order to convey to its buyers that he was Jewish, too, and to do so without vulgar self-advertisement, my father visited the Saalberg headquarters with a Jewish newspaper peeking out of his overcoat pocket. He got the account. But considering what happened later, these commercial triumphs had some rather peculiar consequences. As I have said, my father the Jew did not look Jewish; his partner, Pelz, though "pure Aryan," did. This led several customers to tell my father that he would do well to get rid of the Jew Pelz and thus improve his business even further. It was an invitation that my father was neither willing nor able to accept.

One might suspect that his recovered affluence dulled my father's perception of what was happening around him. But I believe that our relative prosperity did not mask from us the sobering facts of our lives. It may have underscored the gap between what my father was earning and what he could expect to earn abroad and thus subtly reduced his sense of urgency. But how much urgency was realistic? We did not know, and in 1936 our tormentors did not know either. Certainly we never doubted that sooner or later Germany would be no place for us. Meanwhile, though, however temporary, it still was. So between May 26 and June 4, 1936, we took an automobile trip through Germany. The photo album that was my responsibility—it is still in my possession—shows that we concentrated on three lovely rivers in the west, the Rhine, the Main, the Mosel. We did not speak of this excursion as a final farewell to Germany, but such thoughts must have hovered just beneath the surface.

It was a whirlwind tour. My father drove, my mother was the privileged passenger, and I was the historian. Sensibly we took few of our own photographs since none of us was expert; I was in charge of choosing postcards and small albums of local sights to serve as souvenirs and of filling in the names of the towns we raced through. From Berlin we headed southwest through Wittenberg, indelibly linked to Martin Luther's rebellion against the Roman Catholic Church. Then on to Leipzig, where my father and Pelz would go twice a year for its famous trade fair. The national headquarters of the fur business, most of its outlets were still owned by Jewish merchants. As we drove through the district, a name on a marquee, almost shouting "Eastern European Jew," struck me, and I have carried it around ever since: Naftule Dodeles. I wonder where *that* poor man ended up. Then Weimar, the city of Goethe and Schiller, and of the Weimar Republic, now dead and buried deep.

We kept up this breathtaking pace, grasping at impressions as though all these little towns, castles, museums, romantic forests were to be taken away the next day. We stopped at the Wartburg to see Luther's workroom, where he had been hidden as an outlaw while he translated the Bible into his forceful German. As we walked around the castle, we came upon the room where Luther had worked and where, legend tells us, he had thrown an inkwell at the devil. There was a hole in the plaster at one wall about two feet long and wide and several inches deep, with touches of ink at its edges, which, the guide slyly confessed, he and his colleagues regularly renewed to make the visitors' impressions all the more memorable.

We did slow down in Frankfurt am Main, where my father had lived for years before settling in Berlin. He had made good friends there who (as fond inscriptions on the backs of photographs attest) had seen him move to the capital with vivid regret. We visited the cathedral, the Goethe House, the opera house, the railroad station, the statues to Goethe, Schiller, and Bismarck, the old town, and much else, and, with my father as our knowledgeable guide, we found nothing uninteresting.

On the fourth day we resumed our original rate of speed. Driving through Frankfurt's heavily wooded hinterland, we encountered the first and, astonishingly enough, virtually only show of anti-Semitism. As we drove toward a hamlet called Hahn—I have since then tried in vain to locate that miserable hole on maps and in guide books—we were confronted with a large hand-lettered poster proclaiming to anyone who cared to know that Hahn was, and would remain, "clean" of Jews—*Hahn ist und bleibt judenrein.* I suspect that I wanted to burn the place down, but that was clearly impractical. In the excitement of reaching the Rhine and in accord with our unspoken policy of not letting bad news spoil our mood for too long, we pushed the ugly message aside. We drove downstream the celebrated river with its fabled ruined castles and spectacular rocks, including the famous Lorelei. At Koblenz, where the Mosel flows into the Rhine, we turned westward to drive upstream and admired picture-postcard villages and prosperous-looking vineyards. One afternoon, at Cochem, we were having a meal at a pleasant inn when the daughter of the house rushed in, exclaiming: "The gypsies are coming!" We did not stay long enough to witness the encounter, but I have thought since of this primitive emotional response to a feared, little-known enemy who would rank high among the Nazis' victims.

On the tenth day we were back home, and the last entry in my photo album has one name in letters far larger than any others: BERLIN. Triumph at having seen so much so quickly? Relief at being back home? I do not know. I do remember a rare flash of irritation on my father's part. He was telling a guest about our trip and that we had covered two thousand kilometers. "No," I jumped in, "it was only 1,936 kilometers!" My memory produces a quick association to a minor incident that had happened a little earlier. The German post office had issued a new series of stamps, showing a semiabstract representation of the Prussian eagle. Discussing this important news with my parents, I commented appreciatively on the "sterilized" eagles. They tried to inform me that the word I wanted was *stylized,* but I was not to be persuaded. There were times when I must have been intolerable.

In retrospect, this obstinate pedantry looks like a symptom, an obsessive pressure for precision that must have covered some unacceptable wishes. Was I on the way to Tante Hede's "Unfortunately, I am always right"? During these years, when I was about thirteen, I developed little tics that I could neither explain nor resist: lying in bed, I would touch parts of my body—my chest, my flank—with my left hand and then reproduce the number and sequence of my routine with my right. With the passage of time, these ceremonies faded, but they are likely to have been substitutes for masturbation, a resource for a most inhibited youngster. It strikes me, too, as I look back, that around then I became enamored of secret codes and invested much time on them. I designed a system in which scrambled letters could be deciphered only with an elaborate key. Gestures, secrets: I was sending messages to myself that I did not understand.

For me, by far the most formidable adventure of the year, breathlessly anticipated and just as breathlessly enjoyed, were the Olympic Games. I fear that the following pages may bore readers who cannot muster any interest in the spectacle of the best athletes from many nations competing to see who could jump higher, run faster, throw farther. There was so much else to think about in 1936: the Nazi regime had unilaterally nullified portions of the Versailles treaty by starting to rearm and by reoccupying the Rhineland; treaties with Italy and Japan, creating the Axis, came later in the year. But to omit or drastically abridge my Olympic week would be to distort the oscillating balance of the experiences that those trying years deposited in my private history.

My father shone. Exceedingly well informed about sports, he had bought two tickets in 1932 on one of his business trips to Budapest, well before Berlin's Olympic stadium had even been built. Much, of course, had changed in Germany between the time of his purchase of the tickets and the event, but the tickets held good. It turned out to be a move even shrewder than my father could have imagined. Getting ahead of the mob of ticket buyers was canny enough; placing us among a small cadre of colorful, noisy Hungarian fans was cannier still. It meant that my father and I could simply blend in with our surroundings so that we did not have to give the Nazi salute when the Führer appeared or a German was awarded a gold medal. (The ceremony of handing out the medals took place right in the stadium and called for the playing of the winner's national anthem, of which the Nazis had not one but two.)

Conversely, we were safe in supporting the Americans passionately, and we did. Fortunately, they gave us many opportunities to have their hymn roll over the assembled masses, standing quietly or singing along. "O say, can you see . . ." were words whose meaning I could barely guess at (I had had, after all, thanks to Dr. Quandt, no English instruction), but I thought nothing more satisfying than to salute them by solemnly standing up with all the others.

It was a memorable week, and I want to give full weight to the adjective: I remember most of it. The occasional sight of Hitler was a nauseating byproduct. Since we sat almost directly opposite the prestige boxes, on the other side of the big oval, we were doomed to notice all the so-called German dignitaries. When Göring appeared he was hailed with shouts of "Hermann! Hermann!" His bulk, his rows of medals, and his all-too-naked self-importance made him a figure of affectionate fun, a reputation the regime fostered precisely because the real Göring was a thief and a murderer like all his comrades. Fortunately, there was constant activity on the field.

The atmosphere was electric and contagious. More than one hundred thousand sports lovers were packed into a space that accommodated about eighty thousand more or less comfortably. They were ready to leap to their feet at stirring moments—and there were many stirring moments. A good spectator had to command a certain skill: what with all the trial heats to eliminate the weaker competitors, several events were going on at the same time. Preliminaries in the long jump could coexist with the final in the 1,500-meter race.

The hero of the Olympics, and not only my father's and mine, was Jesse Owens. As so often in earlier Olympic Games, the Americans were favored in the sprints, and they did not let us down. But Owens was a revelation. His style of running seemed supremely effortless, in fact elegant. He took home four gold medals, winning each of the events he entered: the 100 meters, the 200 meters, the long jump, and the 4 x 100–meter relay race. There was talk at the time and later—I cheerfully believed all of it—that Hitler, appalled to see a black man showing himself superior to "Nordics," refused to shake Owens's hand. The story has been carefully researched, and apparently there is nothing in it. But from my father's point of view and my own, this is what *must* have happened—it was *morally* true. The swine who were ruining our lives could not have behaved differently. Whatever did happen, there was no denying that Owens had done his bit to puncture the myth of Aryan superiority.

The 4 × 100 relay, in which Owens starred, provided some heart-stopping moments. With their solid cadre, the Americans were expected to win, but how fast could they run? The world's record for the 100 meters was then 10.3 seconds. Anyone who knows anything about running is aware that a quartet of well-practiced and solidly coordinated sprinters can shave off a fraction of time: it all depends on how smoothly a runner passes the baton to his successor. Still, it seemed virtually impossible that the best of teams could break 40 seconds, a boundary set in stone. Owens started and rounded the first curve of the track well ahead of his competitors, and the others were only a touch slower. Thus the Americans, Owens, Ralph Metcalfe, Foy Draper, and Frank Wycoff— three blacks and a white anchorman to break the tape—ran away from the other teams and came in at 39.8 seconds. It is hard to convey the excitement that ran through the stadium: the American foursome seemed beyond nature.

Top row, left to right: my father, my mother's three brothers, Willy, Siegfried, Alfred, and my uncle Samuel Fröhlich. Bottom row: my mother, my mother's parents, Albert and Regina Kohnke, with the former holding my older cousin Hanns, and my Tante Hedwig, known to everyone as Hede, Onkel Samuel's wife.

My mother at 19, looking lovely—and healthy, at best an intermittent state for her.

My handsome father in 1912. He is twenty.

My mother at the piano; her favorite brother, Alfred, ready to play a duet with her.

My father as a wounded soldier in the First World War, in 1915; his brother Siegfried, known as Siege, next to him.

My father, squatting in the center, surrounded by athletes and other "camp followers" of Eintracht Frankfurt.

An Eintracht Frankfurt sprinter breaking the tape, winning the German championship of the 4 x 100–meter relay in 42.9 seconds—an excellent time then. Note the simplicity, even primitiveness, of the track and the stands.

My Tante Esther, one of my father's two sisters, with her husband, Moritz Jaschkowitz; she is wearing her accustomed sad, almost tragic, look. Tante Esther, who with her long blonde hair took the part of Germania in school plays, disappeared into the gas chambers.

So did my Tante Recha, my father's other sister, with her son
Werner.

My Tante Hede—"unfortunately, I am always right"—looking almost pretty, certainly far more fetching than I ever remember seeing her.

Schweidnitzerstrasse, the one-block-long street in Wilmersdorf, in the western part of Berlin, where I spent my first thirteen years, from 1923 to 1936. (Kunstamt Wilmersdorf)

I am with my parents, a mere twenty-three days in the war—still the Weimar Republic.

Being admired by my grandparents in Breslau, the Kohnkes. It is mid-November, 1923; I am about five months old.

The super-good boy, posing a little self-consciously for the camera at the age of three.

Kümmritz 1928

In the hamlet of Kümmritz, some fifty miles south of Berlin, where I spent several health-giving summers as a guest of the Hantels, the parents of our maid Johanna. The Nazis ruined that, too. I am straddling my aggressive weapon.

Kümmritz. I am doing farm chores under the supervision of "Mutti" Hante. Note my necktie.

Johanna Hantel in 1931.

With some classmates in the first grade. This is the only time in my life I have ever been on the extreme right.

My grade school class around 1930. I am once again the good boy, attentive, serious, with my hands folded.

The sportsman at seven and a half.

My grade school class on an excursion. This time I am on the
extreme left, in the first row.

The Goethe-Realschule, where I was a pupil from 1933 to 1938. (Kunstamt Wilmersdorf)

To my mind an extraordinary photo from 1935. A collective portrait of my Gymnasium class with our Latin teacher, Dr. Rose, in the center. My cousin Edgar, with his customary smile, is third from left in the top row. I am the second from the right in the same row, with Hans Schmidt, already an intolerable Hitler Youth, leaning on my shoulder casually, amiably. Pictures do lie!

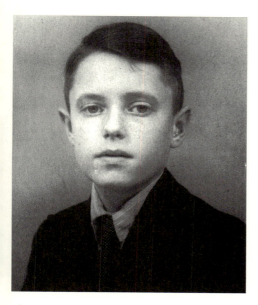

A formal portrait from 1934. I look, I think,
a little distant and not very cheerful.

1937: dressed to play
soccer (which I did
occasionally and badly)
on the balcony of the
apartment to which we
moved the year before.

The Ringbund, my Jewish boy scout troop, in full, if modest, regalia.
I am second from right on the bench. Cousin Edgar stands at left.

Im Namen des Führers und Reichskanzlers

Dem

Kaufmann Siegfried K o h n k e

in B e r l i n

ist auf Grund der Verordnung vom 13. Juli 1934 zur Erinnerung an
den Weltkrieg 1914/1918 das von dem Reichspräsidenten Generalfeld-
marschall von Hindenburg gestiftete

Ehrenkreuz für Frontkämpfer

verliehen worden.

Berlin , den 25.Juni   193 5.

Der Polizeipräsident
I.A.

Nr. K.4830 /35

Speaking of mixed signals: the document—dating from 1935, when
the Nazis had been in power for two years—that notified my Onkel
Siegfried Kohnke that he has been awarded the Cross of Honor,
given to front-line soldiers of the First World War, "In the name of
the Führer and Chancellor of the Reich"!

A snapshot of the Herthaplatz around 1930, where "my" team, Hertha B.S.C., played its home games. The scene of many happy Sundays, including Jewish holidays. (Landesbildstelle Berlin)

Rudolf Caracciola, my favorite racer, in 1934. I "witnessed" his triumphs many times—on the radio. (Landesbildstelle Berlin)

My father's good friend Walther Kern (pseudonym for Walther von Adelsohn), who worked as a sports journalist, announcing the 1936 Olympics. He took me to the England-Germany soccer match in May 1938 and helped immeasurably to make our emigration possible.

The Olympia Stadium in Berlin; it holds glorious, indelible memories for me. (Landesbildstelle Berlin)

The entrance to the Scala, Berlin's best-known entertainment palace, in 1928. A boy's paradise to which my parents took me to see unforgettable clowns and world-famous jugglers. (Landesbildstelle Berlin)

A characteristic shot of a major stamp exhibition in Berlin, the kind my father took me to in the mid-1930s.

1936, the year of the Berlin Olympics, was also the year my parents and I took a quick holiday trip through Germany in my father's Opel, a kind of tacit farewell tour. Here my father and I are posing with the Rhine behind us.

The three cousins around 1937. Hanns, three years older than Edgar and I, is being very grown up with a cigarette between his lips.

In the summer of 1937, Onkel Alfred (extreme right) and Aunt Grace (extreme left), with their blond son Albert (known as Aboo) standing between my grandmother and Tante Hede. On that occasion we set a timetable for exchanging the 1,000-Year Reich for life in the United States.

In the midst of our preparation for "getting out," my father took up bowling (in a Jewish league, of course) and brought home trophies.

Emil Busse in 1934, in his mid-twenties, during the years of his closest friendship with my father. His courageous help to us was still some four years away.

Emil Busse in 1945, recovering in Freienwalde from his anti-Nazi career as an imagined invalid.

Abgangszeugnis.

Edgar Fröhlich

ohn des *Kaufmanns Herrn Samuel Fröhlich* zu *Berlin*,

eboren den *23. September* 19*23* zu *Berlin*, *jüd.* Bekenntnisses,

at der Anstalt *5* Jahre, seit *Ostern* 19*37* der Klasse *O III 2* angehört.

r ist am *15. März* 19*38* nach Klasse *O II* versetzt worden und verläßt die Anstalt,

m *einen Beruf zu ergreifen.*

lligemeine Beurteilung: *Sein Betragen war einwandfrei. Sein geistiges Streben sowie die Beteiligung am Unterricht waren ausreichend.*

eligion		Chemie	
eutsch	*genügend*	Biologie	*genügend*
steinisch		Zeichnen und Kunstunterricht	*nicht genügend*
riechisch		Musik	*genügend*
anzösisch	*genügend*	Leibesübungen	*genügend*
nglisch	*genügend*	Kurzschrift	
eschichte	*gut*		
dkunde	*nicht genügend*		
chnen, athematik	*genügend*		
ysik	*gut*	Handschrift	*nicht genügend*

merkungen: *Versetzt in die 6. Klasse (Oberstufe). Das Zeugnis berechtigt zum Eintritt in die Oberstufe der Oberschule.*

Urteile für die Leistungen: 1 = sehr gut; 2 = gut; 3 = genügend; 4 = nicht genügend.

Berlin= *Wilmersdorf*, den *24. März*

Ed. Quandt
Ober-Studiendirektor

Huber
Klassenleiter

o. H. 28.
. 11078. ● Din A 4. — 4000. 1. 38.

Dordruck für die Oberschulen für Jungen.

A document as amazing as the one awarding Onkel Siegfried the
Cross of Honor in Hitler's name: my cousin Edgar's final report card
from the Goethe-Schule, dating from late March 1938. It records
his promotion to the sixth class (even though his grades were for the
most part "'genügend," which is to say Cs) and, on the same page,
notes that he is leaving school "to take up a profession." Actually, of
course, he is being expelled for being a Jew.

My passport, issued on April 21, 1939, which allowed us to emigrate. It shows my new middle name, Israel, courtesy of Nazi fiat, and a big red J, for *Jude*.

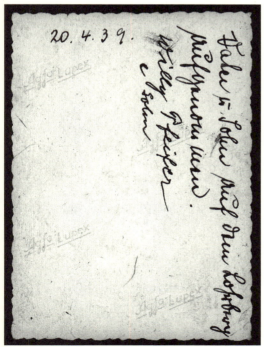

An inscribed photograph that one of my father's oldest friends from Frankfurt days, Willy Pfeiffer, sent as a token of friendship on April 20, 1939, a week before we left for Havana. That the day was Hitler's birthday makes this testimonial all the more emphatic.

I drew this map, showing our daily progress and two aims, one immediate and one remote: Havana and Quincy, Florida, where Onkel Alfred and Aunt Grace lived. Defying the somber realities and our often desolate feelings, I am punning on our name, Fröhlich, to characterize us as a gay, or happy, or cheerful family.

Walking up the gangplank to the Hapag steamer *Iberia*, on April 27, 1939. I am half hidden by my father. Behind me our friend Walther Kern, my mother, and her brother Onkel Siegfried.

My parents in Havana, March 1941. I have already been in the United States for two months, waiting for them. My father's white linen suit was almost de rigueur in the heat.

A liberating moment for me. In the summer of 1945, during an evening at the Institute of World Affairs in Salisbury, Connecticut, I am talking to fellow students and, with two other refugees from Hitler sharing my platform, I break my silence about Kristallnacht for the first time—after seven years.

The Pergamon Altar (2d century A.D.) in Berlin, before and after. A
favorite haunt during my childhood, its being devastated by Allied
bombers, like so much else in my native city, did not, when I first
learned of it after the war, move me to compassion.

Graduation day at Denver University, June 1946.
I am flanked by my proud parents.

My father never made it in his new homeland for all his efforts, but
some refugees did very well. Here, in May 1960, are my Onkel Willy
and his wife, Gertrude, with their car, fins and all.

I admired other Americans, notably the gold medalist in the decathlon, Glenn Morris, an American Indian. Participants in that ten-sport ordeal, who have to do their running, jumping, and throwing in the course of a mere two days, must be exceptionally versatile athletes. And Morris excelled in more sports than his rivals. Impressively, between throwing the javelin, running the 100-meter dash, doing the pole vault, and the rest, Morris would lie down on the grass in the middle of the stadium under a blazing sun and, in full view of us all, put a towel over his head, perhaps to concentrate, perhaps to nap. Winning the final event of the decathlon, the 1,500 meters, almost totally exhausted, he brought in a world's record. Only an American, I thought, without troubling myself with outstanding athletes of other countries, could be so composed and so energetic at the same time.

Unfortunately, many German athletes also did well enough to win an array of gold medals. I took them all as virtually personal insults. Granted, the Germans were nowhere near supreme where it mattered: in the Olympic stadium, where the traditional track and field events were fought out. And I doubted, as did my father, that most of the Germans' medals had been honestly earned. With running and jumping it is very hard to cheat, but when it comes to announcing where a discus or a javelin has landed, partisan judges, if they are astute enough, can fudge results, even in front of an army of amateurs watching from the stands. This is a ripe field for sports paranoiacs.

We were disappointed to be told later that we had seen what we wanted to see: corruption was not so widespread as we had been pleased to believe. Thus in the shot put, in which the American Jack Torrance was the clear favorite, the victory of the German Hans Wöllke seemed to us highly suspect until we learned that Torrance, though a great competitor, had been injured before he came to Berlin and was never in the running for a medal. It remained true, though, that the German athletic establishment manipulated the Games to swell their total number of victories by adding marginal events like women's gymnastics and yachting, in which they were strong, and really irrelevant "sports" like arts competitions. When the Games were over the Germans came in first, well ahead of the United States. It was a propaganda coup for Hitler's Germany, but true sportsmen—I include my father and myself among them—were unimpressed.

Some events, of course, like the 1,500-meter race, which no German had a chance of winning, were politically neutral. Along with the 100-meter sprint, there had long been something special about the so-called metric mile, and this race was no exception. The American Glenn Cunningham, though he ran with an awkward stance, was the favorite, and he led the field most of the way until he was caught on the last lap by the New Zealander Jack Lovelock, a brilliant tactician, who set a world's record.

All this excitement paled before the women's 4 × 100–meter relay, in which a confidently expected German triumph turned into a tearful embarrassment. The German foursome had consistently outrun competitors in earlier track meets and seemed virtually unbeatable. They were equally strong in each position; in contrast, the American relay team, though respectable, boasted only one outstanding runner, Helen Stevens, who had won the gold medal in the 100-meter race. Hitler was in his box, and it depressed me to think that the loyal German Amazons, no doubt adorers of the Führer, would win this one for him.

My father, sitting next to me, was no less dejected as he held his stopwatch poised. He took some pride in his precision in timing races. An experienced observer of track and field events, he showed me that, because sound travels much more slowly than light—I remembered the thunderstorms—one must start clocking a race not when one hears the boom of the starter's pistol but when one sees the smoke rising from it. The final of the relay started and went according to predictions; the German women were quick to take the lead and widened it with each passing of the baton. The Americans trailed in second place some distance behind. Then, as the third German sprinter passed the baton to the anchor for a dash to sure victory, something went wrong. As long as I live I shall hear my father's voice as he leaped to his feet, one of the first to see what had happened: *Die Mädchen haben den Stab verloren!* he shouted, "The girls have dropped the baton!" As Helen Stevens loped to the tape to give the Americans yet another gold medal, the unbeatable models of Nazi womanhood put their arms around each other and cried their German hearts out. A number of years ago, in a brief reminiscence, I wrote that seeing this calamity "remains one of the great moments in my life." I can endorse this judgment now. Schadenfreude can be one of the greatest joys in life. Splinters such as these in a time that gave me little pleasure provided instants of pure happiness.

History has a way of spoiling, or at least complicating, the best stories. It took me some years to recognize the political side of this bracing event. The Olympic Games had been staged by the regime with an eye to world opinion. It had secretly decreed that "spontaneous" outbursts of anti-Semitism were to cease—until further orders. And the Americans, too, I was sorry to learn, had played the political game, on their hosts' terms and to their hosts' advantage. They had cravenly denied places to the only two Jews on their team, both 100-meter specialists, Marty Glickman and Sam Stoller, as fit as the two sprinters who replaced them in the 100-meter relay. The villains, and let their name be recorded, were the chairman of the American Olympic committee, Avery Brundage, and the coach responsible for the race, Dean Cromwell. I am glad in retrospect that I knew nothing of this in 1936. It would have tarnished my unqualified idealization of the United States.

Hormones Awakening

In one of his more problematic aphorisms, Freud contended that biology is destiny. I can certify that biology had its way with me even though I was under such severe pressure that anything and everything seemed to matter more than sex. I had to keep my balance amid the anxieties that were my daily fare—the possible risks of harassment at school, the unresolved question of my future, and, worst of all, the avalanche of assertions, pouring over me from every conceivable source, that I (like all Jews) was a blot on humanity. In this atmosphere, my hormones were not exactly raging, but they came to announce themselves as I grew to be thirteen or fourteen, and with increasing urgency.

I had no opportunity to engage in erotic play, not even in the groping experimentation I learned in the United States to call necking. My school was a boys' school, a lyceum for girls was blocks away, and there was no interchange between us; my three girl cousins, from Onkel Samuel's side of the family, came our way rarely and did not tempt me at all. In the absence of any chance for activity, my fantasies grew ever more florid. Greedy for information, I soaked up whatever wisdom I could from a precocious schoolmate and from books. That schoolmate, who I believe came to the Goethe-Real-Schule later and left before I did, was, I think, called

Mamroth. He is slyly confidential in my memory, with fat, somewhat blurred outlines, a little greasy. But he also seemed to be exceptionally well informed about matters of vital import to me. He told me that he had seen his mother naked in the bathtub, a bit of wickedness that struck me as bold beyond imagining, let alone wonderfully, terribly obscene. My parents subscribed to a slick monthly called *Uhu*, which contained in each number a tasteful photograph of a lovely nude, and I could hardly wait until the next issue came along so that I might continue my studies. That was art, but Frau Mamroth in her bath was life.

Mamroth also introduced me to an array of bawdy short poems, most of them limericks, all of them examples of an apparently inexhaustible series retailing the sexual adventures of a female innkeeper on the river Lahn—*die Wirtin an der Lahn*—and of her intimate circle. They were doggerel of the most primitive kind and largely featured couplings that were marvels of athleticism and penises of historic size, fortitude, and resilience. One limerick I remember was about a young man who, trying to prove the strength of his member, put it on a railroad track and derailed a train.

I write of these adolescent orgies of the mind with a sense of detachment, but at the time these poems, or the vision of a nude Frau Mamroth, made my cheeks tingle with agitation. And with fear: it was around this time that I told my mother I would never get married if I had to do *that!* Her precise answer eludes me after all these years, but I retain a distinct sense that she reassured me: *that* was not really so terrible after all. Surely, frail as she was, *that* appears to have given her a good deal of satisfaction. Perhaps so, but I found it virtually impossible to visualize my mother, this fragile and respectable ninety-pound bourgeoise, engaging in it. Most teenagers have that difficulty, I know, but I must have shied away from visualizing such activity with particular energy.

Yet in some ways I courted knowledge. On occasions— rare because I was horrified and ashamed as much as attracted—I would stop at a display stand to look at the *Stürmer*. True, Streicher's filthy rag showed only Jews as sexual predators, but at least he could not leave sex alone. Another source of excitement, far less guilt-inducing and far more picturesque, was a plaster bust displayed in the window of a beauty salon on Xantener Strasse, which I often passed on the way from Schweidnitzerstrasse to my cousins'. The bust, tinted in roseate hues, sported an elaborate hairdo, which did not interest me, and one lush, round, bared breast, which did.

The most satisfactory educators, though, were books. My parents had hidden some informative literature in our buffet. They had locked the door to the cabinet, but because I was alone on many afternoons after coming home from school, my father in his office or traveling and my mother helping out in Tante Hede's store, I had, once I had located the key, free access to these inexhaustible informants. They included several books on prostitution in Berlin (or did I see them elsewhere? No matter, I saw them), and I can still visualize photographs of whores with their skirts raised to show that they were wearing nothing underneath. Instructive in other ways (I am almost embarrassed to admit this, since it is so commonplace) was a multivolume dictionary I grazed for dirty words. Not all my explorations panned out; some of the esoteric terms from which I had anticipated a fine thrill turned out to be the names of exotic flowers or rare ailments. But a patient—or, rather, impatient—scholar, I came upon some rewarding definitions.

What was dirty about a word—its meaning or its reception? I was led to this question by an amusing anecdote that my father had gleaned from a journal for stamp collectors: exasperated during a quarrel, one man called another a philatelist, and the man thus stigmatized sued for slander. Was he right to go to law or, since the word after all is only a fancy term for "stamp collector," should the complaint have been summarily dismissed? Something of a youthful philosopher, I thought about the story a good deal and meanwhile went on hunting.

Another source, to which I returned over and over to savor favorite passages—the charms of familiarity were almost as intense as those of discovery—was a respectable sex manual by a Dutch physician, Theodoor van de Velde. It was *Die Ideale Ehe* which, of course, I read in German; its English version, *Ideal Marriage,* had a long run in the United States and was for years offered as a dividend by the Book-of-the-Month Club. I recall sixty years later that it had pages upon pages on biology and human sexual organs, which I skipped, and much material on hygiene, which I stayed with only long enough to pick up the hackneyed truth that one's penis or vagina should be clean. The best pages by far, at least for me, dwelt in loving detail and lyrical language on sexual foreplay and a variety of positions in intercourse. There must have been a dozen of these, and van de Velde was graphic enough to make it easy for me to *see* what the couples were doing. Whatever they did, there was at least one more or less acrobatic kind of coupling that promised joys appropriate to men and women of many shapes, ages, and physical condition.

Van de Velde was a moralist: he advocated equal sexual pleasure for both partners. Because he believed that the husband is bound to be far more experienced than his wife—of course, the couple were married, and to each other!—it was his responsibility to lead her gently up the ladder of excitement to eventual fulfillment. To reach this goal, the husband, according to van de Velde, had a rich array of stroking and nibbling at his disposal, including soft kisses on his wife's breasts, shyly offered. If necessary, he might even fleetingly assist her to achieve the wetness required for a smooth junction. I have not looked at *Ideal Marriage* for many years, but I am sure that I would remember if van de Velde had ventured into the more unconventional ways of giving and getting pleasure or had even glancingly considered homosexual lovemaking. He was, as I have said, a moralist, and as such gave himself strict limits.

In the absence of real adventures, I became a frustrated voyeur. Walking or riding my bicycle, I would spot an attractive young woman elevated from the mass of mediocrity by her pretty face, her lovely legs or, best of all, her well-filled sweater. I would fall in love at once, but I was an inconstant Don Juan, capable of dropping my favorite in behalf of another within a few minutes. No masturbation, no erotic dreams, yet. Only an indistinct longing, concrete but unfocused, which I kept to myself. I never told anyone, not even my parents, about the X-rated films playing in my mind, nor did I ever discuss them with my cousins. As I have said, I wanted information and with my sly secretive methods assembled a good deal of it. But I wanted to know more, wanted to know what all this inner turmoil was really about.

It may seem odd that I never turned to my father for help. I doubt that I reasoned about this, but I must have believed that however liberal my parents' willingness to be candid with me, sex education was not part of their pedagogic program. After all, they had firmly drawn the line on June 30, 1934, during the Nazis' purge, and had never explained the meaning of *Lustknabe*. I must have supposed that they would fail me if I attempted to discuss my cravings with them.

An incident that occurred in 1940, while we were refugees in Havana, confirmed that my discretion had been justified. We were living with some distant relatives in a house in Almendares, a lower-middle-class residential district some distance away from the center of the city but easily accessible by bus. One evening I had been in town, probably at a cheap movie with friends, and was returning late on one of those rattling wrecks of a bus so typical of Havana in those days. During the Batista dictatorship, most public employees, whether bus drivers or mailmen, were shabby to a degree; only the soldiers, mainstays of the regime, were sleek: clearly,

that is where the money went. With their new, light tan uni-
forms, well-pressed trousers, clean black shoes, and neat
caps, they looked prosperous and self-satisfied.

That evening, a swarthy young soldier sitting behind me
asked me the time. I had acquired enough utility Spanish
to understand what he wanted but still felt insecure about
my command of his language; I lifted my left arm over my
head and showed him my watch. I came to my stop and got
off; so did he. I had to traverse a very long block to reach
my house, a walk in total darkness that I had often taken
without incident. Not this time. The soldier, several steps
behind me, called to me, and I, all innocence, stopped to
find out what he wanted. What he wanted was sex. The
niceties and delays of preliminaries were evidently beyond
him; he grabbed my right hand with his right and with his
left began to fumble at my pants. This was enough for me; I
tore my hand from his and ran home at top speed. He did
not follow me.

The house was silent, asleep, and, upset as I was, I did
not dare to wake anyone. Yet I was deeply upset. Had that
pervert been attracted by something in my demeanor or by
my smooth, clear, open face? Was this the reason—I was all
of sixteen—that I had never had any kind of sexual adventure, even preliminaries, with a girl? Was I somehow one of
them? When morning came and the fear and confusion of
the night before would not leave me alone, I decided to report
the incident to my father, hoping for some reassurance in my
anguish. I was to be let down.

I did not directly beg my father to dispel my anxieties and
in fact ended my recital with a touch of bravado: "Of course,
I was never in any danger," I said. "People like that are all
cowards, aren't they?" Far from giving me the answer I
craved, not hearing the desperate tone in my question, he set
me straight. Loving as he was, he was distressed by my experience, but it did not occur to him that the last thing I
wanted was a bit of technical instruction. Some homosexuals,

he said, are very tough, and I had been lucky that nothing untoward had happened to me. Neither he nor I pursued the matter further.

I suppose one should not overstate the impact that a single instance of parental obtuseness can have on a panicked adolescent's future, yet I cannot help thinking that my father could have saved me a fair amount of brooding. Perhaps the incident had been somehow triggered by me! A few years later, when I was in graduate school at Columbia, I recounted my self-doubts to a sensible psychiatrist in New York, and he settled matters decisively with a single question: "When you have fantasies about sex, what do you think about?" I replied without hesitation: "Women," and that was that. At sixteen, I had failed to work my own rescue by failing to interrogate my responses. Perhaps my interest in psychoanalysis—assisted self-help—began at that moment. Be that as it may, this ugly episode confirmed belatedly that I had surely been right not to have appealed to my parents three or four years earlier to assist me in steering my way through the shallows of awakening sexual needs.

Why have I decided to give so much space to these intimate matters? One need not be an adherent of Freud to concede that early sexual experiences are bound to leave some mark on a person's erotic history and, with that, his adult character. Every individual's road to maturation is of course unique, but it is likely to show a certain family resemblance to untold numbers of others. I cannot tell how representative I was, but I shared the life history of thousands of Jewish adolescents in Nazi Germany who had somehow to come to terms with their hormones amid massive slanders of their "race" and mounting threats to their survival, threats which were in themselves, not so subtly, offenses to their manhood or conviction of desirability. The regime, with the sufferings and humiliations it imposed on young German Jews, must have disturbed and delayed our sexual development in troubling ways. I do not know how others coped, but as for me, here is yet another instance of how, in the mid-1930s, the outer world disrupted my inner life.

In view of my later engagement with psychoanalysis, another, much earlier encounter with the erotic belongs here. I no longer recall precisely how old I was, but one day I came upon an article in one of the many magazines we subscribed to. The author was waxing indignant about one Dr. Sigmund Freud, who apparently believed that a mother nursing her infant experiences some sexual sensations. This, the journalist charged, was a shameful denigration that dragged one of life's holiest relationships into the dirt. I had little idea just what or who was being condemned, but the writer's vehemence intrigued me; the thought that sexuality, whatever that meant, should invade presumably innocent acts like breastfeeding was a notion I could hardly grasp but that seemed to hold untold possibilities. Sometimes, I suppose, reading too can be destiny.

S I X

Survival Strategies

One early afternoon in the spring semester of 1961—I had been teaching at Columbia for more than a dozen years—I was in my office in Hamilton Hall, writing a lecture. I was teaching a two-semester undergraduate course on the French Revolution and Napoleon and liked to revise some of it every year. We had just reached 1805, the early days of France's First Empire, when Napoleon was nurturing plans for invading Great Britain. His scheme was fanciful, almost utopian; it was to lure British warships from the Mediterranean and eastern Atlantic waters to the West Indies and, after playing hide-and-seek with them around the islands, to dash back to the Channel, where French flat-bottomed boats would carry soldiers to English soil unprotected by Britain's time-tested barricade, its navy.

I had never been much interested in military or naval history, but this sequence of events intrigued me as a prelude to the historic destruction of the French and Spanish flotillas at Trafalgar and Admiral Nelson's death. That memorable exit had been as foolhardy as it was heroic, for he showed himself on board within range of French gunners, his medals aglint in the sun. Poring over a detailed map of the Lesser Antilles, I was suddenly possessed by an impulse as intense as any I have ever known, as inexplicable as it was irresistible.

Helplessly, like a somnambulist, I let myself be dragged along. I put down my pen, put on my jacket, walked across the Columbia campus, took the subway down to 34th Street, and walked to Gimbels (yes, New York had a Gimbels then). There was a certain method to my madness: I had chosen Gimbels (I might almost say that Gimbels had chosen me) because it had a sizable, well-stocked stamp department.

I knew somehow that I was in the right place. Back at Columbia, studying the islands where the French and English had played their deadly game, the names of Barbados, Grenada, St. Kitts & Nevis had won a strange hold on me. What had brought me to the counters at Gimbels was an imperious question I had put to myself: Why are you sitting here working on a lecture when you could be collecting stamps? Where it had come from and why it was so compelling were conundrums, but it had come, and it *was* compelling. At Gimbels's stamp counters, like a voracious but oddly knowledgeable beginner, I bought supplies: a pair of tweezers, a magnifying glass, hinges, empty pages on which to arrange my purchases after my own design, and, of course, stamps. I had collected British colonial islands before, and, with an understandable association of ideas, the names I had been reading just a half-hour before suggested British islands in the Pacific, notably North Borneo and its neighbors, such as Sarawak. I ranged from counter to counter, album to album, like one hypnotized; all sense of time had fallen from me. Then I suddenly remembered that I was due to attend a doctoral examination. I hastily paid for my loot and rushed uptown in a taxi. Inevitably I was late, murmured some excuse, and, my mind on other things, professed to be listening to the questions and answers. Unexpected and uninvited, my past had erupted into my present, with great force.

The episode had consequences: I started to collect stamps with much of the fervor I had displayed for this pastime in my childhood. And it taught me something important about my six years in Nazi Germany: living there I had developed strategies for survival designed to keep me as sane as possible in the madhouse into which the accident of birth and the perversity of history had thrown me. Since these strategies were in place by 1936, this is a good place to drop the thread of chronology and examine them.

Surely my parents were a refuge, an island of order and reason just by being there. We had one another, and even if my mother was less accessible than my father, she belonged to the team from which I drew more comfort than I realized at the time. To come home and close the front door of our apartment was to shut out the world outside, at least to some measure. My father lowered the tension in which I increasingly lived by reassuring me that I was as good a person as I hoped I was and feared I was not. Don't believe anything they say on the radio and write in the newspapers, he often reminded me, and I half believed him. His caution, uttered with conviction, gave me at least some distance from the daily round of slanders.

The little disrespectful antigovernment jokes that my father, along with many others in his predicament, liked to tell were soothing as well. I recall an untranslatable pun. Walking with me past a kiosk selling the latest newspapers, he glimpsed a headline that amused him. The night before, Hitler had given a speech on the international situation and voiced his confidence in the peaceful resolution of all issues dividing the major powers. Lengthy passages from this self-serving fairy tale dominated every front page, and one of them headed its lead story: *Ich aber glaube an einen langen Frieden*—But I believe in a long peace. Putting together the second and third words of this declaration of faith, *aber* and *glaube,* my father pointed out, gave you *Aberglaube,* which is German for superstition. This was pretty feeble stuff, no more than a single brick for the protective wall we were trying to build up against the hoodlums running our lives.

Jokes, told in a low voice and a safe place, were our pathetic weapons. What does the ideal Aryan look like? As tall as Goebbels, as slim as Göring, as blond as Hitler. Or: what happens when Hitler, at the wheel of his purring power machine, runs over a dog near a farmhouse? A little abashed, Hitler instructs a couple of the S.S. men riding with him to apologize to the owner while he waits in the car. Some time passes, and at last the envoys return, laden with gifts: a crate of apples, a basket of plums, a brace of sausages. The Führer, astonished, asks what happened. "We went into the house," one S.S. man reports, "and said, 'Heil Hitler! The dog is dead!'" Such wit would win no contracts for aspiring stand-up comedians, but it meant a good deal to us. We knew that exchanging these jokes was like pitching paper airplanes at a tank, and it is hard to believe, or to convey, how much relief such levity brought us, if only for a moment. Whatever rationality we could rescue lay in these little improvised festivities. We could briefly shake off our tormentors and show our spirit, as my father had done when he jumped up in the jam-packed Olympic stadium and shouted, "The girls have dropped their baton!"

I perfected my strategies without thinking that I was doing anything of the sort. In fact, "perfected" gives me too much credit. These strategies, so to speak, presented themselves to me, and I made the most of them. They show, each and all, the disproportionate significance of the apparently trivial in personal life even in the midst of an emergency.

The first of my strategies was stamp collecting. It had begun very modestly; I was eight or nine when my parents gave me a stamp album. That album was clearly intended for a rank beginner: its paper was cheap, its pages were printed on both sides with squares either empty or adorned with crude replicas of stamps. The highest values in a set, 10 marks, 5£, and the like, were usually lacking; the makers of the album had reasonably assumed that they would be beyond the pocketbook of a collector willing to entrust his treasures to so rudimentary a receptacle. To make the album all the more delectable to me, it already had a number of stamps pasted onto its pages. I, too, "pasted": for some months, not knowing any better, I glued the stamps I was given in the appropriate places. Only after my philatelic knowledge grew a bit more refined did I abandon this barbaric practice and carefully place stamps on their pages with hinges.

I was thrilled with this present and began to beg stamps from relatives and friends. My father, who carried on a sizable foreign correspondence, was my most reliable source. But soon, as much to his surprise as to mine, he began to take a more than paternal interest in my new hobby. Beyond offering benevolent support by buying and hoarding stamps for me, he started to collect on his own, and in earnest. I greatly benefited from his late-born fixation: more adequate albums and more expensive stamps came my way; philatelic journals and specialized catalogs (my father was nothing if not thorough) became shared resources. While I amassed an unpretentious collection of stamps from British colonial islands—I have already mentioned North Borneo—he concentrated on German stamps, on hard-to-get issues like a set featuring the Zeppelin, and on misprints—an inset printed upside down, a wrong numeral in an inscription. These rare errors are the joy of every serious stamp collector, especially when he discovers them himself. I was lucky enough to be one of these minor Columbuses. In a set of 1935 commemorating the anniversaries of three great German composers, Schütz, Bach, and Handel, one small printing of the Bach stamp gave his birth date as 1635 instead of 1685, an error hard to detect. If there is something a little crazy about this feverish scrutiny, I found it immensely absorbing, and that, after January 1933, was the point of it all.

My father's craving was politically neutral. When, for the sake of completeness—and collecting is little more than the aspiration for philatelic closure—he persuaded himself that he needed a block of four with Hitler's hated face on it, he would buy it. Hitler four times! All this activity was exhilarating, but it became more exhilarating still once we started going to stamp exhibitions together to see how major collectors displayed their spoils. These virtuosos of philately had reached summits of sophistication of which my father, let alone I, could only dream. Their pages bore no printed titles or indications of where stamps must be placed; all were lettered by hand, and the stamps themselves were not even hinged (fastidious collectors found the slight traces of a hinge on a mint stamp annoying) but set into little glassine strips complete with a black background to set off each gem. Nor were they crowded together, and the expanse of blank paper on each page bespoke a kind of opulence reserved for the few. We were astonished, a little intimidated, but ready to be instructed by our betters.

I did not resent my father's invading my turf. Anything but hostile, it only cemented an alliance already close. We did things together, understood each other perfectly. That he had real money to spend and I, with my allowance, just a few pennies was only natural. He was a businessman, I was a schoolboy. And as time went by we worked out a division of labor that satisfied us both: my father bought whatever stamps he could afford, while I started to concentrate on an inexpensive but fascinating specialty: German inflation stamps.

After the First World War, what with the occupation of the Rhineland by foreign troops, social unrest often degenerating into violence, and extortionate reparations payments, German currency began to slide in value, at first at a measured pace and by 1922 at a breathtaking rate. In the album that my mother compiled to record my growth, I found an entry that documents the spectacular decay of the mark: on November 10, 1923, the cost of transporting my baby carriage from Berlin to Breslau when we visited my grandparents was 2.5 trillion marks, the cost of a taxi from the station to our apartment, 2 trillion. True, when I was born four and a half months earlier, I was ushered into the world for $20, but that was because my parents had some American currency to spend.

During this vertiginous decay, stamps were susceptible to the general inflation, and the central post office in Berlin could not keep up with the demand for stamps of higher and higher denominations. They could overprint stamps with the legend "100,000 Marks" or whatever it cost to send a letter on a given day, adding a bar to obliterate the original denomination. But by 1923, this method proved too cumbersome, and the central office took to telephoning major branch offices in Cologne, Hamburg, or Munich to instruct them on what new values to print and what typefaces to use. Officially, all stamps issued from Königsberg to Stuttgart should have looked precisely alike, but a sharp philatelic eye could detect minute variations, allowing a collector to identify the city in which a particular stamp had originated. When Germany's miserable fiscal tragicomedy came to an abrupt end on December 1, 1923, with the introduction of a new currency, post offices had untold thousands of unused stamps left on their hands, which, as they entered the market, were traded as almost worthless.

This was my opportunity. I got inflation stamps for practically nothing and, a specialized catalog by my side, sorted them out to construct my own pages just as I had seen done at the exhibitions. It was an ideal situation for a young collector with limited funds. I could display my originality and keep solvent at the same time. Unfortunately, in the turmoil of emigration, this collection was lost, much like my early efforts at literature. But it had served its purpose. I have noted that my parents and I formed an island of order and reason, and the infatuation with stamps that my father and I shared was, it seemed, something of a fortification on that island, granting a certain immunity from outside pressures. When he and I walked around an exhibition together, we were anonymous: we looked and behaved like respectable stamp collectors, and no one would guess that we were detested Jews intruding where we should not be. No doubt these excursions generated a false sense of security all the time that we were haunted by frightening fancies that someone might unmask us. But this was all we had.

If stamp collecting was a stratagem that worked well for me, sports provided still more diverting raptures in both senses of the word: they entertained me, and they fixed my mind on matters remote from the German inferno. Both reached down to the core of my nature; both sublimated raw desire. To be gratified by completing a set of stamps with an unexpected find or discovering an unusual cancellation was a child of the hunting urge: it seemed to me only natural that virtually all serious stamp collectors were men and that my mother should take at best a benevolent but slightly amused interest in seeing her two men hovering over their acquisitions.

Sports, of course, were less genteel. Early in the century, William James had proposed, in his famous lecture "The Moral Equivalent of War," that the expenditure of energy on peaceful pursuits might give innate human pugnacity an alternative to its destructive expression, but his hope has rarely been fulfilled. As the history of sports abundantly shows, far too often rivalries driven to their utmost pitch or invested with local patriotism or national arrogance have seduced competitors and spectators alike to regress to the ferocious animal we all are beneath our veneer. Far from civilizing the players and the fans, sports have often brutalized them both.

I have already described the thrilling week my father and I spent at the Olympics. All his life, he enjoyed track and field and called runners his friends. But closest to his heart, certainly to mine, was soccer. At its best, I found, soccer could be a thing of pure beauty. Its notorious low scores have kept it from becoming truly popular in the United States. But uncounted millions across the world reveled then, and revel now, in the fluency of the action, the explosion of an attack, the astute pass of a playmaker that transforms what looks like a stalemate to a scoring opportunity. Soccer fans—and I am one of them—will tell you that a match closing with no score can be an exciting event from beginning to end. The only American parallel is a pitchers' duel in baseball, with a no-hitter providing the utmost in pulse-raising suspense.

Soccer has been likened to ballet, but it is far more im-promptu, far less organized, than that. A coach will train players for specific duties and prepare them for the team co-operation on which victory depends. But for the rest, every moment is new and requires an instant individual response. Hence the kind of attention soccer demands could banish even Hitler from my thoughts—at least during game time.

In my gratitude I am perhaps idealizing the game. There were soccer players—I saw them—who would prefer to aim at an opponent's shin rather than at the ball. And I shared the noisy resentment of other spectators against players who destroyed the flow of the action by pointlessly passing the ball back and forth among each other without gaining any territory or, having run out of ideas, passing it back to the goalkeeper. With equal fervor, we swore at forwards who lost their nerve on the attack, failing to take an easy shot or stu-pidly shooting wide.

My father had become addicted to soccer as a young bachelor in Frankfurt am Main and made Eintracht Frank-furt, as prominent for its runners as for its soccer team, his emotional home. Among the photographs we managed to res-cue from Nazi Germany are several of these players, which he kept through the years. I cannot look at them without fondly recalling this sports-drunk amateur. His conscientious inscriptions on the back of these pictures identifying the per-sonages and their particular achievements speak eloquently of his wholehearted commitment. There are formal group portraits of Eintracht relay teams and of the soccer team with my father in the midst of the assembled athletes; there are action photos—a woman runner breaking the tape in that awkward twisted posture typical of an athlete intent on improving her performance by a fraction of a second, a male sprinter on his way to yet another victory for Eintracht.

A genial and likable man, the kind of dependable partisan that used to be the lifeblood of any sports club, my father was—to give the phrase a benign meaning—a camp follower. In those days, sports organizations were run by amateurs who donated time, and often money, and the athletes who competed under their banner were expected to be amateurs no less. Hence the true fan, like my father, did volunteer work for his club at formal meetings or social get-togethers, loudly cheered for his boys—and girls—at home events, and, even more important, accompanied them into the lions' den at away events to demonstrate much-needed support in the stands and to neutralize at least partially the raucous partisanship of their competitors.

Not all amateurs were impeccable volunteers. The International Olympic Committee, run by men with lofty credentials in the social register, was exceptionally rigid about athletic purity, though its hysterical anxiety over possible scandals itself became a scandal. The most notorious case that occurred during my lifetime was the disqualification of the great Finnish competitor Paavo Nurmi, the long-distance runner who competed holding a stopwatch and who between 1920 and 1928 established twenty world records and collected nine Olympic gold medals. The powers-that-be decided to ban him from the Games of 1932 for taking money for performances, thus making him the lowest of the low—a professional. This snobbish legalism irritated my father and me. But actually, German soccer authorities left players a good deal more leeway by winking at undemanding jobs that allowed the players time to train and travel. It was all very innocent in those days, when Nurmi could be branded a great sinner. One need only glance at photographs of the improvised running lanes or the primitive accommodations for spectators to see that, compared with today's sports millionaires, athletes between the wars seem to have lived in another world. And so they did.

When my father moved from Frankfurt to Berlin the year before I was born, he enlarged his loyalties by adopting a new team, Hertha B.S.C., without abandoning his friendships with players from the Frankfurt days. He was particularly close to one Eintracht player, the defensive fullback Willy Pfeiffer, and his wife. In 1922, upon my father's departure, Pfeiffer gave him his photograph inscribed: "To my dear friend." There is nothing out of the ordinary about such a tribute, but a second photograph is a very different matter. It shows Pfeiffer and his young son, dated "April 20, '39"—a week before we emigrated. At such a moment, this kind of affectionate token, looking so casual and yet actually so risky, was a political message. Whatever racial theorists would say, Pfeiffer recognized and saluted my father as quite simply another German whom he had no intention to disavow. The irony of the date—it was Hitler's birthday—cannot have been lost on either of them.

My father's new club was at home in Gesundbrunnen, not far from my Onkel Siegfried's apartment. Its plain but efficient stadium held perhaps 35,000 spectators, and it became my home away from home. One long side of its rectangular grounds had a roof and seats; the other three offered standing room, with waist-high iron bars let into the ground, useful props because as you leaned on one, you could rest your feet. The two short sides, each behind a goal, gave a good view only of the action in that area, and I scorned them, always arriving early enough to stand as close to midfield (in America the 50-yard line) as I could.

My father was as ardent and studious a soccer fan as he was a stamp collector. He subscribed to two weeklies, *Der Kicker* and the *Fussballwoche,* and, like a true squirrel—the fan as collector—he kept all the copies. When we left Germany, we still had two complete runs of these periodicals. They contained the expected: extensive coverage of major matches, interviews with stars, notices of games to be watched for in the coming week, and, of course, complete charts of the standings. More, as a dividend for cosmopolitan soccer watchers, they offered substantial coverage of soccer abroad, principally in England.

The world owes soccer to England, one of the country's least controversial exports. First played in the mid–nineteenth century by boys in the exclusive private schools that the English call public schools, the game was reduced to uniform rules in the 1860s and then became wildly popular among the general population, particularly among those not rich or upper-class enough to watch cricket. England was the model to which other soccer countries looked for inspiration and, later, for coaches; its national team was deemed to be unbeatable, certainly when it had home-field advantage.

Immediately partisan, I embraced an English team: Arsenal, a highly rated London club. Several of its players were regular members of the national team, and Arsenal had numerous championships and equally coveted Football Association cups to its credit. It was an innovative organization, noted for introducing an unprecedented way of positioning its players on the field. None of this deserves detailed attention here; what does is my reason for becoming a single-minded Arsenal supporter. A pure lover of soccer is not likely to pick a team to root for simply because it is a proven winner. More esoteric impulses, at times comprehensible, at times irrational, and always deeply private, determine the team to which a spectator gives his love: a father's partisanship (I certainly "inherited" my father's devotion to Hertha), an appealing player, the colors of the club. But Arsenal? I had never been to England, I knew no English; if I had seen the team in a stadium without a program I could not have told Arsenal from Chelsea or Leeds or Manchester United.

But I needed a reliable champion in my corner, a champion that would distract my attention from a situation in which I was doomed to be a loser.

As I explored the feelings and actions that I had come to recognize as my survival strategies in the Nazi Reich, I readily acknowledged that my infatuation with Arsenal (and only marginally less so, for that matter, with the local team Hertha B.S.C.) must appear as eccentric as my preoccupation with stamps from a half-savage country far away that I would never see. Hence I found it a considerable relief when my friend Stefan Collini, who teaches at Cambridge University and knows more about rugby than I do about soccer, introduced me to a memoir by Nick Hornby, *Fever Pitch*, which must be the best study ever written about the peculiar symptomatology of being a fan.

Probably I found the book particularly engaging and persuasive because the team to which Hornby became enslaved was my team, Arsenal. But beyond this, I accepted his diagnosis as simply valid. He fell in love—it is his term—at the age of eleven, the year he entered the local grammar school, suffered a bout with jaundice, and, most painful of all, watched his parents' marriage disintegrate. "I would have to be extraordinarily literal to believe," he writes, "that the Arsenal fever about to grip me had nothing to do with all this mess." And he wonders whether other fans, "if they were to examine the circumstances that led up to their obsession, could find some sort of equivalent Freudian drama": granted, "football's a great game and everything, but what is it that separates those who are happy to attend half a dozen games a season—watch the big matches, stay away from the rubbish, surely the sensible way—from those who feel compelled to attend them all?" The question leads him to a "theory of fandom as therapy." For me, too, fandom was therapy, though Hornby and I were battling different traumas.

When I became aware of Hertha in around 1929—I was six—the team had undergone tantalizing years of near-triumphs: four times in succession, from 1926 to 1929, it had reached the finals of the national championship, and four times it had been beaten. Hertha B.S.C. looked like the Boston Red Sox of Germany: a fine team on paper afflicted with a curse. And then, in 1930, my father, my two cousins, and I listened intently to our small and crackling radio to see if Hertha, in the finals for the fifth time in five years, would win the championship at last. And so it did, in a nerve-wracking game, by the tight score of 5–4. A year later it repeated its victory. I can still recite the names of most among the players on Hertha's roster (my cousin Edgar could recite them all). By the time I began to attend Hertha games on my own, the glow of this unique past still hung over the stadium even though the club's time of greatness was passing.

The atmosphere at the Hertha stadium was boisterous but not menacing. Fans did not storm the field and mainly liked to shout out good-natured insults or the names of favorite players. When Hertha scored a goal, or sometimes from sheer exuberance, its supporters would intone a chorus, "Ha! Ho! He! Hertha B.S.C.!" Not exactly imaginative but heartfelt. And when the other side scored *its* goals, especially when it was the chief local rival, Tennis Borussia, fans of the Others raised their own shout, a malicious parody: "Hi! Ha! Ho! Hertha is K.O.!"

One favorite roar went "Hanne! Hanne!" to spur on the most gifted among the Herthaners, Hans Sobek. It was right, I thought, and only to be expected that my father knew this great man. In a silver cigarette case dated "Christmas 1924," a gift to him from the Pfeiffer family, more than a dozen athletes, some of them national champions, had incised their names, and Hans Sobek was among them. Not all these friends of the 1920s remained my father's friends in the 1930s.

One of them, the outstanding hurdler Heinrich "Heiner" Trossbach, whose signed photograph my father kept among his souvenirs, refused to shake his hand when they met at some sports event in the Nazi days. Even Sobek lent himself to the new regime during those years by allowing himself to be appointed to a post in Berlin's sports radio.

For me, as for everyone, Sobek was a dazzling playmaker; though a forward, he was better at preparing goals than at scoring them. He was playful in the best sense of the word and sometimes in the worst; with exemplary ball control, something beautiful to watch, he could dribble his way past several opponents to set up yet another scoring chance. But when I saw him most regularly, he and the century were in their thirties, and more often than before he allowed himself to be seduced by his mannered technique, forgetting that his task was to serve his team rather than his reputation as a stylist. In fact, the most vivid memory I have of Hertha on the field is of Sobek handling the ball with almost erotic concentration, as though he were alone on the field. When this happened, or when he chose to give an artistic exhibition rather than take a shot at the goal, I would join thousands of fellow fans and yell an anguished "shoot!" I suppose that I found these little explosions particularly welcome because they provided a safe escape from the near-silence the Nazis had imposed on me.

One special reward of soccer was to play Monday-morning quarterback on the way home. We left, as we had come, via a nearby subway, so tightly pressed against our fellows that, people said, if a rider was unable to put his feet on the floor, he would be carried in this floating posture for several stations. This choking crowd scene put me into a situation as hazardous as it was enjoyable. Here I was, officially the scum of the earth, wedged among Berliners with whom I had little if anything in common and who might have maltreated me if they had known who I was. But for me, game analysis conquered private anxiety; I joined the mob offering it with finesse and loudly voiced claims to expertise. Had a Hertha forward missed an obvious chance for making a goal? That damned Hanne had failed to convert his best chances! Had the goalkeeper let a shot past him that he could have stopped? Geelhaar, the Hertha goalie, an old regular well liked by the fans, did not escape criticism when criticism seemed deserved, but since he was usually so reliable, he was entitled to an off day. Highest on the agenda of these authorities was the competence—or, far more often, incompetence—of the referee. Especially when the game had gone badly, there was a consensus, which I naturally shared, that without his stupid interventions or his equally stupid inability to see a visiting player's foul right before his eyes, Hertha would surely have won the game it had just lost.

It is, I trust, obvious that I have written these pages about sports not to write about sports. A fixation on basketball or tennis is only too familiar to us all. But for me, as it dawned on me many years later, sports were more than an adolescent's commonplace infatuation. Nor were they convenient stimulants to fill some inner void of boredom. I was never bored; often I wished I had been. True, I caressed fantasies about my own, wholly imagined, sporting prowess: in my daydreams I was as elegant as Hanne Sobek and more productive. In reality, I played a little soccer and did so rather poorly; I was too worried about injuring my kneecap to develop the fearlessness necessary for competent work on the field. But as I have said, from 1933 on, the reason for my posture as a fan was that sports could serve as a screen blocking out the oppressive world of Nazi Germany. With its regular weekly rhythms, the soccer season provided a certain continuity at a time when we lived, as it were, from day to day, Nazi decree by Nazi decree. That sports brought me even closer to my father only added to its charms. "Ha! Ho! He! Hertha B.S.C.!" It almost seemed something to live for.

My father figured in still another strategy, far less formidable than the two I have just discussed, but with a certain flavor of its own. I have already confessed my craving for chocolate. (It is one of the malicious tricks of fate that I of all people should have picked up a mild case of diabetes in advanced years which puts sweets out of bounds.) Chocolate pudding, with vanilla sauce, of course, was my mother's department, and she did not stint on the quantities she produced for me. And my father brought me chocolate from downtown Berlin in little white bags which he deposited in the right, always unlocked, turret of our buffet more or less above the copy of van de Velde's *Ideal Marriage* hidden in the lower cabinet. Our overpowering piece of furniture thus provided, as a psychoanalyst in a sprightly mood might see it, oral pleasures at the top and genital pleasures at the bottom.

The pristine white bags contained two sorts of chocolate. One held little stamped pieces made on a form—chimney sweeps, soldiers, four-leaf clovers. They were delectable. The second sort, called *Borke,* or bark, was even more so. The pieces were round, with deep rills circling the surface, looking, as the name suggests, like small segments of trees. They melted easily, and a bit of the chocolate, like a very small, very thin, and very tender leaf, would stick to my fingers. This was the most delicious of all my strategies.

I do not claim that I invented the idea of strategies for survival; surely thousands of adolescent German Jews, girls as much as boys, must have adopted strategies of their own to suit their needs and their opportunities. Without such mental escape routes, their disorientation, their sense of self under unremitting assault, would have been beyond bearing. Sly and gross in turn, the anti-Semitic propaganda campaigns, calculated to drive us to despair, were so incessant, so repetitious, so all-embracing that it was nearly impossible to escape them. Our confidence that whatever we heard from official sources was a lie could give us some relief, but it was temporary at best.

At our worst many of us must have found rather alluring what Anna Freud has called identification with the aggressor. We know this maneuver from sensational cases past and present: the American colonist who, abducted by Indians, chooses to stay with them rather than return home; the victim of a kidnapping who falls in love with her captor. To be in the victors' shoes just once, to relax our vigilance and the constant need to keep our critical faculties alert to dismiss ever new libels, to march with the triumphant enemy, to have someone to admire beyond reason!

I find it repulsive to confess the very existence of such an obscene aberration, even to think about it, however fleeting and occasional it must have been. A moment's thought would have exposed such notions as not merely unworthy but wholly impractical. The handful of right-wing Jews who in 1933 thought it possible to reach an accommodation with the Nazis soon learned that they had foolishly misjudged the intentions of the Führer. And so, if the seductive appeal of surrender crossed the minds of some of us, the notion would have been promptly rejected. But after three or four years of trying to stand erect in the whirlwind of hate and contempt, the most resilient among us found that keeping our defenses in working order was exhausting.

To be sure, many German Jewish families had what looked like a way out: to acknowledge, even to insist on, their Jewishness. The relatively small minority that subscribed to the ideology of Zionism made a radical break not just with the Third Reich but with all of Germany, and this gave them a place to stand. The parents who sent their children to Jewish schools from 1933 on might know little of Jewish culture, Jewish religion, Jewish history, but they knew enough, they believed, to give their children, and themselves, a secure identity that could take daily insults as just another instance of barbarism. What, they would ask, could you expect from the goyim? The Nazis sang *Heute gehört uns Deutschland, morgen die ganze Welt*—Today Germany belongs to us, tomorrow the whole world. For their part, these Jews at least could say defiantly, in the prescient words the journalist and historian Robert Weltsch wrote in 1933: "Wear it with pride, the Yellow Star!"

It is arguable whether this affirmation, be it ethnic, religious, or nationalistic, made life easier. But for my parents and for me, cherishing our Jewishness was not an acceptable option. We did not want to be Jews by Nazi edict; their definition of our "race" was just another lie that we repudiated as unhistorical and unscientific. We did not think of ourselves as members of a chosen people, divinely selected for glory or for suffering. Whatever our pious fellow-pariahs might say, we could not make ourselves believe what we did not believe, though it might have been comforting at the time. And so, my strategies, facing the temptation of committing treason or of professing what I thought to be nonsense, had to do double duty.

SEVEN

Best-Laid Plans

For a time it seemed as though 1937 might bring what 1936 had promised: an alleviation of pressure on Germany's Jews, or at least no intensification. Yet this was the year in which our family made concrete plans to get us all out of the country, displaying a trust in our arrangements that in retrospect appears naive. How were we to know, when the Nazis themselves did not know, that they would drastically speed up their timetable of persecutions? The road to Auschwitz was never straight or foreseeable. But these arguments have seemed nothing better than lame excuses to the critics of German Jewish assimilation I later encountered, only too often, in the United States. For them, our situation had been obvious from the start; German Jews, they said (to borrow a phrase from the historian Charles Beard), without fear and without research, had been culpably blind in the face of spectacular warnings and had sold out to an irresponsible fantasy known as the German-Jewish symbiosis.

Self-appointed commentators, especially decades after the fact, found it all too easy to reprimand German Jewry collectively: "And you still thought, after the Nürnberg Laws and other horrors, that you were Germans?" But we *were* Germans; the gangsters who had taken control of the country were not Germany—*we* were. Like everyone else interested in this dismal controversy, I learned about the indictment of German Jewry by the great scholar Gershom Scholem; a Zionist from his youth, he had argued since the early 1920s that the notion of a German-Jewish symbiosis was sheer self-delusion. The Jews, he insisted memorably, had loved the Germans, but the Germans had never loved the Jews. Yet my parents and I did not think we were living a delusion. Granted, our Germany had taken refuge in exile or was living underground at home, and resistance to Nazi oppression appeared to be impossible. But we believed that the Nazis had no right to impose their perversion of history and biology on us.

The most formidable obstacle to fathoming things to come was doubtless the very insanity of the Hitlerian program. "It was all in *Mein Kampf*" has long been the litany of our detractors, who, without an inkling of what uprooting oneself meant and how hard it was to read the signals, reproached me or my parents for not having packed up on January 30, 1933, and left the country the next day. But Hitler's threats were so utterly implausible that we regarded them as unreliable guides to future conduct. They were literally incredible. Germany, after all, was the most civilized of countries; it was the country that, next to the United States, was the haven of choice for Eastern European Jewish emigrants looking for a tolerant society relatively free of anti-Semitism. France had shown its anti-Jewish leanings in the Dreyfus case; England seemed an almost impermeable society; the German record was one of a centurylong, almost uninterrupted improvement of relations between its Jewish and gentile populations. Inflated, demagogic political rhetoric was one thing, actions by a government compelled to live within an international community, in the improbable event that Hitler ever took power, would necessarily be quite another.

We now know that, tragically, Polish Jews influential in their communities shared this illusion, and it would prove fatal to them. In the fall of 1939, as German troops were sweeping through the Polish countryside, Jews clustered in

villages and small towns debated just what to do: flee eastward toward the Russians or stay and put their faith in the
Germans. The Russians were a known, and hated, quantity;
the Germans had retained the good reputation they had established in the First World War, when German occupiers of
Polish soil had shown themselves civilized and generous to
the Jews. Sadly out of touch with the world, Jews in Poland
faced with the necessity for immediate action, even after
Kristallnacht and other Nazi pogroms, allowed their memories of the good Germans of the past to overpower their incomplete and inaccurate information about the evil Germans
of the present. The result was Nazi mass murder.

Paradoxically, in some ways the decent Germans who
kept in touch with us and, when we needed them, helped us
did us no favor: they made the Nazis' promise of a new Aryan
era appear all the crazier. In 1937 the Nazis themselves had
no clear agenda of just how to proceed against the Jews. They
had eliminated "Jewish influence" on high German culture,
on the press, on finance, in government, in much of business;
for the rest, they were going to get rid of Jews by exporting
them. The "final solution," to use one of their damnable eu-
phemisms, was only a glimmer in the eyes of the most fanatical anti-Semites.

I stop for a minute to consider what I have written. We
were not so stupid, not so deluded, certainly not so treach-
erous as we have been judged to be, usually by other Jews:
this theme has been a subtext through these pages and now
has emerged as a central preoccupation. It is no doubt legit-
imate to read much of this memoir as an apology for my
parents and for my fellow-German Jews. But it is an unapol-
ogetic apology. After spending years pondering this matter, I
remain convinced that our critics have never quite understood our dilemmas in the 1930s; most of them never even
took the trouble to try and understand them. Is this a self-
serving plea? I think not, but I must let my readers decide.

113

In late May of 1937, I had a sobering experience that showed me with unmistakable clarity the resourcefulness and the ruthlessness of the thugs we were up against. I was at home, listening to a speech by Goebbels, whether from sheer curiosity or on the principle Know Your Enemy I cannot now recapture. In what was billed as a major address, Goebbels was speaking to his loyal fellow Nazis and thus was sure of impassioned approval. Chicago's Cardinal Mundelein had recently made disparaging remarks about the Nazis—he instantly became another American hero of mine—and in response, Goebbels brashly trumpeted a string of shocking anecdotes about sexual offenses committed by German priests and nuns. It was a weirdly gripping performance; Goebbels, a seasoned snake charmer, commanded a hypnotic voice that he played like an instrument, a counterpoise to Hitler's ravings. As he exhibited one revolting clerical perversion after another, his audience, wholly in his power, broke out in a chorus of shouts of "Pfui! Pfui!" and "Hang the traitors!" It was as though I had encountered the iniquity of the enemy with full force for the first time, and I told myself that the road ahead would be hard.

During these months, whatever our unfounded hopes, my family had grown weary enough of the drumbeat of racist propaganda and economic chicanery to recognize that it was high time to act. Our opportunity came with a visit from Onkel Alfred and Aunt Grace. The occasion for this particular transatlantic voyage was the failing health of my maternal grandmother, who, sedate and old-fashioned, had a room in Onkel Samuel and Tante Hede's apartment. She lives in my memory as a gentle old lady who kept to her room a good deal. A severe diabetic, she gave herself insulin injections twice a day and watched over her diet with fastidious care. One of the memorable features of her room to me was a food scale with a square flat top on which she would put her permitted piece of bread and then spread her permitted piece of butter on it. I must confess that I was her favorite; my two cousins, whom of course she had numerous chances to observe, often displeased her, but I never gave her grounds for disapproval. I suppose it would have been better for me in the long run if she had sometimes found fault with me, but my family seemed engaged in a well-intentioned conspiracy to nourish my illusion of being merely perfect.

The plan we formulated during this crucial visit from overseas seemed reasonableness itself: the boys would move to the United States first, starting with Hanns, followed by Edgar and me. Our parents and Onkel Siegfried would join us soon after. The priority given to Hanns was natural: he would complete his gymnasium education the following year, and Edgar and I could come over shortly afterward, as soon as practical. No one considered keeping us two in the Thousand Year Reich until we had completed our stint at the Goethe-Real-Gymnasium in 1941: that much at least we had learned. There was a sense of urgency in our talks, but no panic. A year more or less, we believed, would make no difference.

In response to this agenda, Edgar and I began to study English around the end of 1937. We had the same teacher but saw her separately. She was a woman of a certain age, slender, well tanned (it seemed to me), and with an attractive, somewhat husky voice that may have been the result of heavy smoking. Her apartment was full of books. I liked her immensely, and I sometimes wonder what happened to her in the Holocaust years. Was she too herded onto a cattle car and sent to the gas chambers? I cannot remember her name, but I harbor the faint hope that she may read this—although she would be quite elderly by now—and write to let me know that she, too, made it out. It is terrible to think of her as a mere name on a casualty list, part of my past that seems dead but is not resolved, a piece of achingly unfinished business.

I took to English as though it were my mother tongue that I had mysteriously forgotten, as through a sudden amnesia—the kind that used to affect people on daytime radio serials—and was reclaiming at remarkable speed. I fell in love with the language and came to regard it as an incomparable vehicle for expressiveness. I still do and take the many pages I have written in English as so many tributes to what I like to call my adopted first language.

The self-confidence my teacher awakened in me allowed me to venture, boldly and precociously, into English literature. The first book I bought to assuage my imperious appetite—I found it on one of those carts that had supplied me with detective novels for some time—is still a treasured possession. It was a cheap, badly mauled paperback copy of Shaw's *Saint Joan*. The previous owner, whose grasp on English was even shakier than mine, had marked a number of less familiar words with German equivalents. This little venture has made me value Shaw's play, impressive as it is, beyond its merits. I suppose I have always needed spotless heroes, whether in sports or in drama.

One other book I read in those days, *Gone with the Wind*, I did not dare tackle in English. For me, the novel will always be *Vom Winde Verweht*, and I can still produce its opening phrase: *Scarlett O'Hara war nicht eigentlich schön zu nennen, aber* . . . which, in the original, reads, a little more economically: "Scarlett O'Hara was not beautiful, but . . ." I thought it was a wonderful novel, but that I was compelled to resort to a translation suggests how limited my resources in English still were.

As my teacher and I became friends she would lend me books in German as well as in English. One of these was to destroy our relationship on a dismal and discreditable note, thanks to Edgar's inability to keep his mouth shut and his parents' unbecoming straitlacedness. I had noticed on her shelves a novel, *Fabian*, by Erich Kästner. Unlike the Kästner books I knew and loved, this one had no illustrations. (I still like to think back with pleasure on the witty illustrator of the others, Walter Trier.) My Kästner was a highly popular author of delightful, imaginative children's books; one of them, *Emil und die Detektive,* became a minor classic that would be adopted as a staple text in the United States for courses in elementary German. The idea of a Kästner for grownups intrigued me—I was then fourteen and in the midst of my sexual researches—and she lent me the book without warning me that it might be too "mature" for me. She was not by temperament a censor and thought she could count on my good sense. To my pleased astonishment, *Fabian* contained sexy scenes told in light-hearted prose, and I shared my find with Edgar. I should have known better: Edgar the security risk was true to form. Tante Hede was outraged, Onkel Samuel predictably followed her lead, and they forbade any further lessons. To my surprise, my parents went along with this draconian edict.

Why this yielding to the decrees of Tante Hede, who was the dictator in her domain but whose intrusions into our family life my parents had usually withstood? *Fabian* was admittedly, as Kästner himself noted in the preface, not for teenagers, and he warned of suggestive scenes. But I suspect that my parents thought it best if I studied English more intensively than I had. For my final four months in Germany I attended a course that did somewhat improve my linguistic competence. Thus scantily equipped did I come to the New World. But a foundation for later mastery had been laid down.

The dismissal of my English teacher came at the end of 1938, and much had happened in the preceding months that made my acquisition of English all the more imperative. To be sure, not all my experiences in that terrible year were messengers of travail to come. As before, my life went on its complicated and contradictory way. Twice I went to the Olympic stadium to watch soccer games that any sports-loving person would have agreed were truly important: the England-Germany match in May and the final of the German championship a month later, my last visit to the stadium for more than two decades. The latter event had its own interest; an upstart team, Hannover 96, held Germany's unrivaled champions, Schalke 04, to a draw, 3–3, even after overtime. I did not return to the reprise.

In any event it was the England-Germany match that remains a high point in my boyhood, and large fragments of it have stayed in my memory. I owed my ticket to a friend of my father's whom he had known in his Frankfurt days, Walther von Adelson, a respected sports reporter who wrote under the name of Walther Kern. He had covered the 1936 Olympics for radio and now, two years later, had managed to obtain two precious tickets for a much ballyhooed encounter that had been sold out many months before. My father, with his characteristic paternal altruism, gave up his seat to me, but this time I did not enjoy the cover our Hungarian fellow enthusiasts had given me in the Olympics; I had only Kern with me as a friendly presence.

As I looked around at the crowd of 100,000 spectators huddled close and electrified by the magnitude of the event they were about to witness, it occurred to me that I might well be the only Jew in the stadium. Soon, though, the match itself claimed my absorbed attention. England won it convincingly by 6–3, displaying dazzling football. What I relished most was the artistry of Stanley Matthews, England's right outside forward, who made a complete fool of the German defense. He is the most elegant player I have ever seen, and when several years afterward I read that he had been knighted, I thought that this represented simple justice.

The controlled German press was permitted to admire the English team unstintingly. Some of it was, of course, tendentious; to admire so splendid a victorious opponent was a form of self-praise: it was no discredit to have lost to such master technicians. In another event, though, which gave my father and me another joyous present that year, Nazi journalists were less generous. It was the second Joe Louis–Max Schmeling bout, for which my father stayed up until about

118

three in the morning to get a blow-by-blow account live from New York. Two years earlier, Schmeling had beaten the "Brown Bomber" soundly, but this time, the "lower race" had its revenge: Joe Louis knocked out Schmeling in the first round. To a man, German reporters insinuated that this would never have happened if Schmeling had not been hit below the belt. Curiously, German sportswriters were the only witnesses to have seen this low blow. We did not care; for my father and me, the American's victory was quite simply good news.

Such exhilarating moments were thin fare in 1938. The Nazis had invaded Austria in mid-March to the frenzied cheers of Austrian multitudes and virtually no protests from foreign governments. We followed events with mounting repugnance and alarm. Radio Strasbourg, our sole resource for truthful newscasts, reported on the well-organized, unchecked, government-sanctioned thievery that was robbing Austria's Jews of property and livelihood and on the thousands of imaginative Austrians who were committing acts of spontaneous sadism designed to tread Jews almost literally in the dust. So much for the city on the beautiful blue Danube! Casually formed crowds forced any Jew they could lay their hands on to recite passages from *Mein Kampf* or to clean up anti-Semitic graffiti on walls and sidewalks with a toothbrush. And these were among the milder humiliations Austria's Jews had to swallow. The suicide rate among them in Vienna and other Austrian cities rose to spectacular heights. We would have been troubled even more if it had occurred to us that this legally sanctioned lawlessness was only a dress rehearsal for worse pogroms soon to come.

Month by month, at times it seemed week by week, the Nazis tightened the noose around our necks, precisely when other countries were making it only too clear that few of us were welcome within their borders. By the thousands, citizens of the civilized world—politicians, preachers, artists, editorial writers—voiced sincere indignation at the persecution of the Jews in Germany, but with few honorable exceptions they fell silent when it came to rescuing the victims. The highly touted and justly maligned international conference at Evian, held in early July, was depressing proof that goodwill by itself was impotent. There was much humane talk and no humane action. Countries as population-hungry as Canada or Australia were not really interested in the likes of us. And the United States showed itself unwilling to relax its strict quota system—after the *Anschluss,* when Austria's quota was absorbed into the German one, it amounted to little over twenty-seven thousand a year. A bitter joke made the rounds among us, helpless witnesses to worldwide professions of helplessness: Evian spelled backwards reads "naive." My faith in my American idol, F.D.R., did not waver—in politics, too, I needed my heroes. But to us the absence of concrete steps after the summer of 1938 was a direct menace. Escape was all that mattered, but who would have us?

More and more German Jews not yet hounded out of a job or a profession were dismissed. One particular instance touched me directly: a much older friend, Walther Schreiber, who lived in our apartment house, had worked for thirty years at the Berlin headquarters of the Dresdner Bank, but on April 1, 1938, he was "retired" for being a "non-Aryan." In the same month, the few remaining Jewish students in the Goethe Gymnasium were permanently dismissed; not even I, the son of a wounded and decorated war veteran, was spared.

The act was not without its irony, an echo as late as 1938 of the mixed signals that had made it so hard for us to stabilize our expectations. I no longer have my report cards, but my cousin Edgar's widow has sent me his last one before he was expelled with the rest of us. This *Abgangszeugnis,* dated March 24, 1938, records that his work in the previous year, though scarcely brilliant, had been adequate, so that he had been promoted to the upper school, to his sixth year. At the same time, on the same page, an entry noted that Edgar was

leaving the school *einen Beruf zu ergreifen*—to take up a profession. One of the two signatories was Dr. Quandt.

What are we to make of this document? Was it a euphemism designed to preserve on the record as few tracks of the
school's iniquity as possible? Was it a bureaucratic formula
as meaningless as such formulas often are? Was it a last
shred of decency on the part of an institution that had been,
considering its circumstances, remarkably free of bigotry? All
these together, I think: I have no intention of waxing sentimental about my school, but I read this astonishing text as a
final farewell to civility, not without at least a twinge of regret.

But I had larger worries than unriddling the purport of
this gesture: what was I to do with myself? My parents took
my involuntary leisure as an opportunity to find a place that
would train me in something useful, no matter what, as long
as it was a skill I could transport to new climes. My mother,
already a skilled seamstress, worked to improve her sewing;
my Tante Hede studied to make herself, of all things, into a
pastry cook. This was a choice that we three cousins could
only applaud: it gave us ample opportunities to sample her
output, and we relished her failures scarcely less than her
successes.

It is only too easy to overdo the humorous side of these
pathetic self-improvement schemes. Here were two middle-
class women, two among thousands, who were willing to con-
template working abroad, not in their own store or at home
keeping house, but as employees somewhere—anywhere.
Even my aunt, inflexible and domineering, could respond to
the realities of 1938. I had a first taste here of how German-
Jewish women would prove themselves, once they were safely
abroad, far more adaptable than the men.

As for myself, I signed up for a trade school which, in
retrospect, must have been a kind of reform school, where
casualties among Berlin's adolescents could be parked and

perhaps turned into useful, employable citizens. It was such a hellhole that I remember nothing of it except that I felt wholly out of place, wholly alone. I left it after about a month and unexpectedly found employment as an apprentice to a dental technician. Because my employer and his wife were deaf and mute (though their daughter was not) it was part of my job to answer the telephone and negotiate with customers on the line. I was also the delivery boy to dentists who had not abandoned their unfortunate Jewish technician. My bicycle came in handy. I worked hard and learned little, although my employer tried to initiate me into his mysteries. My mind was elsewhere, and the one bit of knowledge I have retained is that if you coat your hands with ice-cold water, you can reach for an object immersed in boiling water without burning yourself if you do it quickly. The single positive feature of my dull and wearying routine was the daughter of the house, who was young, attractive, and busty. I included her in my pantheon of desirable beauties though I spoke to her only on matters of business. Such were my love affairs in those days: one-sided, silent, and quite unconsummated.

Meanwhile, the government multiplied anti-Jewish regulations and issued new, ever more stringent anti-Jewish edicts. Even a partial list may give the flavor of the time: in April, Jews were forbidden to conceal their share or their partnership in gentile enterprises and with gentile associates. In the same month, all Jewish fortunes above 5,000 marks had to be registered with the Commissioner for the Four-Year Plan, which is to say Göring, and officials began to draw up registers of Jewish property across the country. Confiscations seemed only a matter of time.

Then on July 1, the new order—or disorder—intruded on our own lives more massively than ever before: Pelz, the "Jew" Pelz, threw my father out of their firm without compensation and, given the Nazis' legal and judicial system, without recourse. My father had long wanted to liberate himself from his partner, but now that partner, secure in the protection of the "laws," anticipated him. We started to live off our savings and redoubled our efforts to leave Germany. I too was enlisted in the effort, going to consulates to pick up forms to fill out, typing up applications as well as I could. The dining table became our office, serving a single purpose: emigration. During the summer, we applied for residence in Great Britain.

Other portents proliferated and at unprecedented speed. In June, Munich's largest synagogue was torched. Late in July, Jewish physicians were forbidden to treat gentile patients and deprived of their status as doctors. They had to call themselves *Krankenbehandler,* those who treat the sick, and to replace the time-honored black-and-white enameled plaque posted near the front door of their houses with a new one with a specified color—I seem to remember it was blue— to let the public know that there was a mere Krankenbehandler within. In August the forced sales of synagogues in various German cities at ludicrously low prices went forward. In September it was the Jewish lawyers' turn: like Jewish physicians, they were stripped of their gentile clients and their professional title and called "Jewish consultants" instead. Meanwhile, in mid-August, in a classic exhibition of Nazi chicanery, the government compelled Jews to add Israel or Sara to their names—the passport issued to me in April 1939 attests that this was not a momentary whim. Then in early October the passports of German Jews were differentiated from those of "real" Germans by a red *J* stamped on the front page, an ingenious Swiss suggestion that the Nazis adopted with alacrity.

It is at such moments in my story that the criticisms with which I have dealt before start all over again. Why didn't you leave then and there? Why did you wait for atrocities that were bound to come? Was your father paralyzed (and I am not inventing these snide inquiries) by fear that he might make less money abroad? Such questions seem reasonable enough if one disregards the world in which we lived and the efforts we made to escape. What makes these hostile questions all the more infuriating is that they barely conceal a knowing and derisive undertone: Whatever happened to you served you right. Why did you—or your parents and grandparents—betray your Judaism and try to assimilate to a culture that did not want you? I have already raised the key response with two questions of my own: who would have us, or in time? How could my father, with no foreign language and no marketable skills, live abroad at all?

The year 1938, then, was the grimmest we had experienced so far in Nazi Germany. These are times on which I do not like to dwell, and as I noted at the beginning, I have found that thinking back on them only revives my old rage. But I dare not slight the last months of 1938 and the first months of 1939; the events of that half-year were to force my life into a new direction. They were events, too, that most severely tested what I earlier called my preparation for the Hitler regime.

As our surroundings grew measurably chillier, we were thrown together more than ever with Tante Hede's family. Hanns, Edgar, and I spent our weekends in one another's company at their place, and I don't think we wasted much time brooding on our precarious situation or possible fate. Our defenses were in place. Hanns had managed to obtain a few jazz records—two or three pieces with Cab Calloway singing raucously—which the Nazis had outlawed. We played them at the low sound level appropriate to activities forbidden in our dictatorship.

Certainly, the Nazi regime fully deserved the epithet *totalitarian* that political scientists bestowed on it. The Nazis put their hands on everything, including music; no minutiae of daily life escaped them. I remember in deepest winter the sound of amplified records floating over our neighborhood tennis courts converted to a rink, where I liked to skate in the mid-1930s. From one day to the next, this rhythmic accompaniment to my greatly enjoyed but relatively clumsy efforts on the ice distinctly changed—no more swing (in the early Nazi days, I had heard the Paul Whiteman swing band at the Scala), let alone jazz. And so, putting a Cab Calloway record on our phonograph, a large heavy box in those days, gave us, even though the risks of detection were minute, a heady sense of being outlaws. More safely, we played table-top soccer with mechanical men whose right legs we could manipulate with a button in the skull; we would shoot a small multicolored and multifaceted wooden "ball" at the opponents' goal. Edgar was not averse to cheating a little now and then, but he was always caught.

The radio, too, proved an unfailing resource—for sports, naturally, and occasionally for a variety show that was strong (we thought) on comedy. We listened to track meets or automobile races with the same vehement partisanship that enlivened our excursions to the soccer stadium. Each of us had his racing hero; mine was Caracciola, who drove for Mercedes Benz. I chose him for the same reason, I think, that I had chosen Arsenal as my team in English soccer: he was a winner. We also liked those comedians who were by and large unpolitical and whose jokes were attuned to minds no more mature than ours. One of their adolescent gags has stayed with me for some sixty years. A team of radio buffoons named *Die lustigen Gesell'n aus Kölln*—the Jolly Fellows from Cologne—was carrying on an inane dialogue about someone who had won an endurance contest by playing the piano for an uninterrupted stretch of 120 hours. *Aber essen muss man ja,* mused one of the funny men, over and over. "You've got to eat, though." With its delicate hint at scatology, this sort of thing broke us up. Let no one underestimate the therapeutic value of this foolishness—it gave us breathing space, no matter how short.

On Sundays our parents joined us. We three boys were sent to the bakery, which punctually opened on that day at 2 P.M. and just as punctually closed two hours later, to buy

125

pastries for us all. Hanns, being the oldest, was entrusted with the money, but in his timid way—which quite disappeared in our animated friendly disputes over sports—he sent us in to do the actual buying. We returned in triumph carefully carrying a large cardboard plate laden with delicious morsels and covered with a pristine sheet of paper, to join the adults for coffee and cake. When the day was fine, we sat outside: my aunt and uncle lived on the ground floor and had a small terrace in the rear of their apartment, complete with an iron-legged table and some matching chairs. When we finished, we would go inside to play rummy. In this mundane way we established a certain soothing continuity with life as we had lived it before 1933.

But we set cards and cake aside when it was time for the news. We would close the windows, draw the curtains, and tune in to Radio Strasbourg. The Nazis had foisted on the populace cheap radios that by design did not reach beyond local stations. Starved for usable information, we resorted to the powerful radio in my cousins' apartment, thus making ourselves guilty of listening to "anti-German propaganda." What we heard was invariably disheartening, but whatever our inclinations to deny reality, we thought it better to know than not to know.

This sort of control was typical of the regime and touched us every day of our lives. It managed to choke off German contacts with foreign opinion, spreading misinformation and plain lies like a toxic fog. It opened people's mail, especially from and to other countries. It reduced the press, we have seen, to a lackey's docility until the media essentially served only to distribute government handouts and the kind of cringing propaganda they called editorials. It inveigled respectable Germans to report on their fellow citizens, even on members of their own family, for making subversive remarks or uncalled-for political banter. It made access to foreign newspapers dependent on the paper's goodwill toward the New

Germany. I recall that as my halting English improved, I tried to buy London papers and found that most of the time only the *Daily Mail* was available: a sad reflection, I thought, on the paper's editorial policy but none the less valuable to me and the rest of my family.

One episode may illustrate how zealously the regime sought to strangle independent expression. In the mid-1930s Emil Busse, a friend of my father's who had worked for some years at Fröhlich und Pelz, got involved in a political quarrel with an elderly, rather ineffective fellow salesman who was a devoted Nazi and, like most of these types, quite humorless. His comparative failure at my father's firm can only have exacerbated his sensitivity to slights real or imagined. One day, seeking to trump Busse by adverting to his youth, he said, *Sie sind mir viel zu grün!*—You're far too green for me! To which Busse countered, alluding to the Nazis' favorite color: *Und Sie sind mir viel zu braun!*—And you're far too brown for me!

Busse's antagonist took this riposte as an insult to his cherished political convictions and denounced him to the Gestapo. Summoned to headquarters the next day, Busse in his perplexity consulted my father, and the two devised a defensive tactic. I can see the two friends scheming to figure out just how to draw the sting of this accusation, a team bound together by Busse's respect for my father's abilities, my father's trust in the younger man, and their shared detestation of the Nazis. After the Gestapo interrogator had ceased yelling at him, Busse meekly remarked that of course he had not said, and would never say, anything of the sort. Actually, he claimed, he had said, *"Sie sind mir viel zu grau*—You're much too gray for me!—I was getting back at him for calling me a youngster."* This story loses in translation, for in German *grau* sounds much like *braun,* and the excuse seemed plausible enough. Busse got away with it, but it was a reminder that in Nazi Germany, jokes were no joking matter.

This is a good place to say something more about Emil Busse, who was to loom larger and larger in our lives. A true Berliner, born in 1909, joining an extraordinary narrative gift to an exceptional memory, he effortlessly carried on the tradition of his city's expressive speech. I have learned much from him about Berlin, about the crystal and china business, about my father. Running a small store in Berlin as a young man, he was impressed by the manufacturers' representatives who stopped by to offer their wares. Far more self-confident than mere salesmen, they struck him as worldly, high in self-esteem as well as the esteem of their peers. Around 1930 he made his leap and began working for my father. Their friendship was strong and lasting, though they continued to address one another formally, using *Sie* till the end. Those Germans!

Forceful and outspoken, a true individualist, Busse was a born anti-Nazi. Quite apart from his detestation of anti-Semitism (his closest associates turned out to be Jews), he had no use for the Nazis' sullen earnestness, their authoritarianism, their self-conceit, and their vicious political ideas. Busse was made for opposition, the last thing the Nazis needed. Not unexpectedly, he was in trouble with the authorities off and on even before the brown / gray episode. Once, during the celebration of some Nazi triumph, when raising a flag was considered a civic duty, he was an exception on his block: no flag. The block warden came around to ask why not. "I haven't got a flag." The block warden promised to find one, and did. Still no flag. Why not? "I haven't got a flagstaff" . . . and so forth. It was not a healthy way to be in the Third Reich, but it was Busse's way. That he would show himself immensely helpful to us when our time of need came went almost without saying.

There were many hours in those days from 1936 on when I faced the world, or refused to face it, alone. I liked my cousins and got along with them, but there was in me, I

128

think, a certain longing for solitude. I have already noted that in the afternoons, when I came home from school, my parents were likely to be out of the house. I used my solitary leisure to read, to write my novel, to construct my puzzles, to play a little piano, to improve my knowledge of sex with yet another glance at the forbidden books. By then, of course, I knew the most rewarding passages virtually by heart, and only the erotic thrill that no repetition can dull sent me back to my favorites.

My reading included Dickens—in German. I had become friendly with our neighbor Walther Schreiber. His son, I believe, was about my age. More important to me, though, was that Herr Schreiber owned the collected works of Dickens complete with the magnificent illustrations by Phiz and others, and that he readily lent them to me. Sometimes, when I think of this friendship, it occurs to me that I was unnaturally grave for my age, as though I had never been really young. This was only to be expected in a household such as mine, and certainly the Nazis fostered qualities like discretion and earnestness that made me appear far more grown up than my still childish mind could have wished.

But precocity had its rewards: it was through Schreiber that I discovered *David Copperfield,* Dickens's "favourite child" and mine, and came to idealize its spotless heroine, Agnes Wickfield, a love I have never got over. Far more than the many other novels I have read, *David Copperfield,* which proved as splendid in English as in German, remains fresh in my mind in virtually every detail. I can name all the characters and visualize their fates. A first love, Freud says, is always the strongest, and this book and its heroine were my first love. Interestingly enough, I shared my taste for Dickens with my mother. One day I came home to see her crying; that troubled me, but her tears, I soon discovered, were for Oliver Twist.

Not all pleasures were literary. Alone, I developed elaborate entertainments in which I took all the parts and played against myself. With our dining room table as a base, I would build up a track, using playing cards to construct a hilly race-course and mah-jongg pieces as its boundaries. Then I would take differently colored round plastic pieces, looking like poker chips, only smaller and thinner, to represent racing cars and propel each of them forward by pressing a larger disk down on them. This was my *Avusbahn*, the miles-long straight avenue in western Berlin, the venue of automobile races. I would win, I would lose—cheating was not allowed—and thus, as I thought at more self-critical intervals, I wasted my time getting through yet another day. While my life, initially so full of promise, was crumbling around me, I moved around our dining table pursuing my racers and played my lonely games.

Then, at the end of September 1938 came Munich, where the British and the French yielded to Nazi blackmail. A crippling lack of military preparedness and haunting memories of the devastating casualties of the First World War gave western statesmen, they thought, little room for maneuver. They looked at the vast Allied cemeteries, the monuments in town squares and college chapels crowded with the names of the dead, and they wanted no part of another war. And the appeasers could rationalize their capitulation with the thought that the Germans had a point in clamoring that the Sudetenland, the largely German-speaking northern slice of Czechoslovakia, should be incorporated in the Thousand Year Reich. That Czech government leaders were not invited to the banquet at which the great powers conspired to give away some of their territory left a bad taste, and so did Munich altogether; the name of the city became a byword for ignominious surrender. Only a few discordant voices spoke up against Hitler's aggressions, most eloquently that of Winston Churchill, who tried to alert the West to the consequences of appeasement. But at the time they found few echoes. It is notorious that when Britain's prime minister,

Neville Chamberlain, returned after the conference at Munich, he claimed that he was bringing peace in his time. Hitler did not share this conviction, or shared it only at the cost of having all his territorial demands met.

Munich was father to the Kristallnacht; without the first, the second might never have happened. Hitler's complete diplomatic victory gave him and the rest of the Nazi leadership a giddy sense of being at liberty to do anything they liked abroad and at home. My grandmother and my cousin Hanns were fortunate. She died in October, and Hanns left for the United States in the same month; thus both were spared the catastrophe that overtook Germany's Jewry the following month.

Kristallnacht followed upon the death on November 9 of Ernst vom Rath, legation secretary at the German embassy in Paris. He had been shot two days before by a young Polish Jew distraught at the fate of his parents who, along with some sixteen thousand Polish Jews living in Germany, had been mercilessly deported a few days earlier. The *Manchester Guardian,* the most consistent voice for decency anywhere in the world, wrote with feeling and complete accuracy of a "brutal expulsion." There was to be worse brutality soon.

Exploiting the event with their accustomed adroitness, Nazi propagandists spread the word that vom Rath's death created such fierce indignation among the German people that they went on a rampage. This version, that Kristallnacht represented a spontaneous response of angry Germans to a Jewish crime, was so fanciful that nobody believed it. The *Manchester Guardian,* like other newspapers abroad, put the word "spontaneous" in skeptical quotation marks. They were, of course, absolutely right: a regime that had made a specialty of the big lie was now promoting one of its biggest lies ever. Local authorities across the country had compiled lists of Jewish stores months before and had the names and addresses of Jewish men on record; in Berlin, some time before this "impulsive" outburst of collective "indignation," Jewish store owners had been compelled to paint their names on their front windows in large white letters. If there was ever a thoroughly organized pogrom, it was Kristallnacht.

I know that the word *Kristallnacht,* the established name for this historic, countrywide pogrom, has been disparaged for presumably trivializing an event in which more than glass was shattered. The best estimate is that almost a hundred Jews were murdered during the riots and more than twenty-six thousand Jewish men were hauled off to concentration camps. Throughout Germany, synagogues were severely damaged or totally burnt out, sacred scrolls desecrated with the peculiar elation and ingenuity that the plunderers brought to their work. Thousands of businesses were ravaged or destroyed, and in numerous cities—Vienna, of course, in the lead—even private houses and apartments were reduced to piles of rubble, with furniture, pictures, clothing, and kitchen equipment thrown around so that they were barely recognizable. There was some looting; particularly stores with portable items like clothing were emptied out. In our neighborhood, a jewelry store was systematically pillaged. But for the majority, the thrill lay in destruction for its own sake.

This wallowing in sheer aggressiveness has made Kristallnacht something of a puzzle. As historians have observed, the regime could have continued to rob German Jews of money, art, real estate—whatever they owned—by "legal" means and without resorting to gratuitous public violence. In an interesting article, "The Kristallnacht as a Public Degradation Ritual," published in the Leo Baeck Institute *Yearbook* for 1987, my friend Peter Loewenberg, historian and psychoanalyst, has offered a persuasive explanation. The pogrom had results that obviously suited the regime's policy: it isolated the Jewish population of Germany even more from their former fellow citizens, and it served to intimidate gentile Germans: attempts to show sympathy for the victims, let alone give them assistance, were dangerous.

But there was more to it than this; Kristallnacht was, as Loewenberg has shown, a degradation ritual, a handy way of realizing the Nazi leaders' most unchecked fantasies about a "race" that to their twisted minds had infiltrated, exploited, and betrayed Germans for centuries. The Nazis' scenario called not just for depriving Jews of their livelihood and driving them from the country virtually penniless but for doing so with the maximum publicity and with actions that would make the Jews feel like the pariahs they had become. An eyewitness report from the American consul in Leipzig, David H. Buffum, which Loewenberg quotes, attests to this sick rapture: "Having demolished dwellings and hurled most of the movable effects on the streets, the insatiably sadistic perpetrators threw many of the trembling inmates into a small stream that flows through the Zoological Park, commanding the horrified spectators to spit at them, defile them with mud and jeer at their plight." By involving bystanders, the Nazis made them into accomplices.

The story of Kristallnacht has often been told, at times in ghastly detail, but I must speak of it because I was there. And I shall continue to use the conventional term because to me, as to most of the witnesses, it conveys far more than its literal meaning. I read it—no, I feel it—as a catastrophe that deepened my rancor against Germany and Germans, already powerful enough, into an indiscriminate hatred that survived long stretches of time quite unabated. These were the years when I weighed the Emil Busses too lightly in the balance.

In the morning of November 10, when a good deal of the damage had already been done, I bicycled to work on my customary route along residential streets and noticed nothing out of the ordinary. Later that morning, my father called to say that there was trouble and that I should come home. I did not ask for details but got on my bike and, following a different course, pedaled through a city that seemed to have been visited by an army of vandals. So, of course, it had, but what made this visitation extraordinary was that these vandals had been set in motion by the regime itself. The route I took on the way back to Sächsische Strasse happened to be through the Tauentzienstrasse, lined on three or four long blocks with large specialty shops. Their façades had been efficiently reduced to rubble, their huge display windows shattered, their mannequins and merchandise scattered on the sidewalk. Evidently more Jewish-owned stores had survived the government's efforts to "Aryanize" them than I had imagined. I kept my head down and bicycled my way home. The aloofness I had cultivated for so long did me good service that morning.

When I reached my apartment house, I met the superintendent's wife at the front door, crying. I asked her what was wrong, and she told me that "they" had come and taken Herr Schreiber away. I parked my bike and rushed upstairs. My father was not there, but my mother told me that he was safe: he was with Emil Busse. I found out later from Busse just what the two friends had done that morning: they had sauntered through the heart of the city to inspect the damage, just two Berliners on a stroll. The scene that most appalled them was the assault on a small hotel on the Spree River, one of the few hostelries still owned by a Jew. The mob had gone through the place methodically floor by floor, breaking all the windows, bursting into the rooms to demolish the furniture, slicing open blankets and pillowcases and throwing heaps of feathers into the street below. It was a barbarous snowstorm, a collective orgy hard to believe and impossible to forget. My father never mentioned this walk to me, nor did we dwell on the pogrom at home. But when I asked Busse how my father had conducted himself during this "casual" walk, he told me that he had been calm and self-possessed. I can well believe it, but I also believe that at this moment a determination was born in him to do anything, no matter how illegal, to get the three of us away from the German nightmare.

Reassured about my father's whereabouts, I decided to do some reconnoitering, unconsciously imitating his actions this day and his determination not to give way to panic. I thought grimly of the one lesson I had learned at the dental technician's: it seemed as though the cold water of my acquired public habits gave me some temporary protection against what I was seeing. I walked over to my cousin's house. The family was there, in misery, Tante Hede tight-lipped, Onkel Samuel weeping. This was not the way my parents or I would respond, but after I saw what had happened to their store, it struck me that they had good cause to lament.

It was pure chaos. If there was ever a commercial establishment that might invite hoodlums to do some enjoyable trashing, it was "Fröhlich" on the Olivaerplatz. Its waist-high glass counters holding stockings, gloves, and ladies' underwear had proved irresistible; they had been smashed and their contents savagely torn to pieces. But the wall cabinets had given the wrathful German people avenging the death of vom Rath even more entertaining targets. One of the cabinets, well over five feet tall, with an array of shallow glass-fronted drawers, had held innumerable fine shadings of thread; the other, quite as high and as minutely subdivided, had contained buttons, with a sample sewn onto the front of each drawer. Both had been ripped from the wall and emptied pell-mell, their contents mingling with glass fragments strewn all over the floor. It was as though the store had been swept by a hurricane.

Many years later I happened upon a contemporary account, a diary entry of November 12 by a young woman who took a walk through this quarter of Berlin two days earlier and came upon the Olivaerplatz. Her account confirms my memory of devastation in every detail. Although it does not identify the store by name, it can only have been Onkel Samuel and Tante Hede's business. It looked "desolate," the diarist reported, "the window pane smashed into atoms, the shirts, underwear, and stockings shredded and strewn across the broken glass, the shelves overturned, the cash register demolished apparently by hammer blows."

Onkel Siegfried never mentioned it, but his property in Gesundbrunnen was also devastated on that day. In a sworn declaration of 1961, which formed part of his case for financial restitution, the daughter of his landlady declared that Onkel Siegfried had been renting his premises from her mother since 1911. It was a small factory with five "doubtless very valuable" kilns for firing glassware and porcelain, a special chimney, and well-organized equipment—special shelves, apparatus for grinding colors and for spraying the glassware and the like—all of which he had to abandon when he emigrated. Across the street, in the deep entrance to an apartment house, Onkel Siegfried had built a dozen glass display cases, each more than six feet high and six feet wide. "In the so-called Kristallnacht, these display cases were shattered after they had been smeared all over with words like 'Jew' etc. I myself have seen the broken pieces on the floor of the entrance hall after Kristallnacht."

The world watched, disapproved, and did almost nothing. In the United States, the public's attention was still focusing on the midterm congressional elections of November 8, and the press was busy assessing its results. Still, diligent foreign correspondents saw the reality and sent their papers unsparing dispatches. Otto D. Tolischus of the *New York Times* walked around on November 10 from early morning—getting up with the milkman, he said—and reported the catastrophe as he saw it. On November 11, in his second story from Berlin, which dominated the front page of the *Times,* he noted that "while a large section of the German population seemed thoroughly ashamed of the exhibition of mob rule, those who participated in anti-Semitic actions had a gay time." The *Manchester Guardian,* which in three or four days ran a dozen stories about the pogrom, spoke with candid distaste of "organized revenge," of a "fanatical government," and of "justice" in quotation marks. The response of Berlin's public, the paper's special correspondent noted, was either apathy or, at best, "shocked amazement." No wonder that in those days, no copies of the *Guardian* were to be found on Berlin's newsstands.

During this reign of terror, it was reassuring to me that the "good" Germans, too, were active: my father was in hiding in Emil Busse's apartment, sleeping on his living room couch. Busse did not need any more trouble with the Nazis but stood ready to risk it. Beyond this, my memory has given out; the rest of November 10 is a blank to me. After my tour of inspection I must have gone home and eaten dinner with my mother. By the end of the day, one thing was plain: the timetable we had so carefully worked out with our American family earlier that year would have to be speeded up, drastically. I do remember that this night I slept soundly.

EIGHT

Buying Asylum

With an effrontery calculated to reduce the Jews of Germany to helpless rage, the Nazis first committed the atrocities of Kristallnacht and then promptly blamed the victims. To transfer culpability from the guilty to the innocent is a time-honored technique, but the rulers of the Third Reich took to it with a zest that astonished even seasoned students of politics. Psychoanalysts have a technical term for drastic reversals of the truth: *projection,* unconscious stratagems that burden others with the flaws or hateful desires one senses in oneself. But this diagnostic term does not apply to the criminals of November 1938. They knew perfectly well what they were doing and relished it. Liberated from all constraints by the craven conduct of the Western powers and supremely cavalier about world opinion, they brazenly reversed the truth.

On November 12, Göring convened a meeting of the Nazi leadership to canvass the position it should take after the damage had been done. With Göring and Goebbels showing themselves, as the latter put it, the most "radical," one after another of the participants put anti-Semitic proposals to the group. They were trying, as Peter Loewenberg has observed, to trump previous speakers: Jews were to be forbidden access to theatres or movie houses; Jews were to be assigned their

own compartments on trains (unless the train was full, Göring suggested, in which case they should stay at home); Jews
were to be identified by a special uniform; Jews were to pay
a collective fine of one billion marks. These men were playing
quite literally with people's lives.

That very day, though some of these rabid wishes would
have to wait, several of them were fulfilled: the fine was officially imposed; the few remaining Jewish stores were closed
or forcibly "Aryanized"; Jews were forbidden to attend cultural events like concerts, films, exhibitions. And, as if to
certify the cynicism of the participants in this conclave, they
decided that Jewish victims of the pogrom not only would be
forbidden to claim reimbursement from their insurance com-
panies but were to pay for, and clean up, the havoc the Nazi
marauders had wrought. On the next day, Goebbels recorded
in his diary with loving detail his triumph and Göring's over
more half-hearted colleagues and crowed over the victim's
plight: "190 synagogues burned down and destroyed. That hit
them where it hurt—*das hat gesessen*." No one could deny
that, especially since the number of synagogues destroyed
was far larger than even Goebbels then knew.

In the immediate aftermath of Kristallnacht, my father,
after taking his terrible walk through Berlin, boarded with
Busse for a few days until it seemed that the "action" was
over. Once he came home, we redoubled our efforts, already
intense, to find a haven. We did what nearly everyone else
in our predicament was doing: we wrote more letters, we visited more consulates, we filled out more forms. Having gotten
hold of some American telephone books, my father wrote to
several people named Fröhlich to see whether he could perhaps find a distant cousin of whom he had never heard, all
in vain.

We hoped for England; given the unbending limitations
of the American quota system, the many thousands who were
ahead of us in line, and my father's unlucky relegation to the

Polish quota, the United States seemed out of reach for the foreseeable future. We had rich relatives, and they had vouched that none of us would ever become a public burden. This was the famous affidavit—the indispensable document for anyone aiming to enter the United States legally. But for all our relatives' goodwill, all their money, and all their exertions, they could not remove the obstacles to our joining them soon.

My father's inclusion on the Polish rather than the German quota was just one more example of how lives could hinge on political deals or bureaucratic decisions, often deals made or decisions taken years before. He had been born in that narrow sliver of Silesian territory turned over to Poland in the peace treaties following the First World War. American law specified that a petitioner for admission to the United States must be classified according not to birth or citizenship but to the country to which his birthplace belonged at the time of the application. According to American immigration authorities, then, my father was a Pole, making him one of fewer than six thousand to be eligible each year. That this provision of the law was sheer nonsense made no difference.

These were anxious days. The civilized world professed deep indignation, even outrage, at the November pogrom. Protestant and Catholic clergy in country after country thundered against it from the pulpit and said prayers for the victims, editorial writers searched for heated adjectives, politicians (especially those with Jewish constituents to think about) bravely shouted themselves hoarse about German iniquity. It all sounded very good to us, and—I have protested against this before—completely hollow. None of this verbal onslaught led to the action we needed: a place to go. There were ugly scenes at the German border, some of them faithfully reported by Radio Strasbourg, which had become indispensable to us. At the Dutch frontier, as frenzied German Jews pleaded for asylum literally on their knees, the government doubled its border patrol to keep out all the Nazis' victims; not that the Dutch approved of the pogrom, but the Netherlands was loath to irritate its big, muscle-rippling neighbor. The Dutch were to learn in May 1940 that this appeasement did not spare them a Nazi invasion.

The international press was virtually unanimous in its condemnation and indefatigable in its reportage. American, British, French, Dutch, and other newspaper readers had ample information about outrages not just in Berlin and Vienna but in smaller cities and towns across Hitler's Germany. But those of us on the spot were deeply dismayed that these reports contained virtually no suggestions about just how to rescue Germany's Jews. A trickle of applicants, of course, continued to find refuge here or there, and a Canadian official was quoted as saying that Germany's Jews might be settled in the unpopulated northern reaches of his country. Politicians elsewhere mentioned even more esoteric spots like Kenya or British Guiana, but nothing came of these schemes. In 1939 a bill introduced in Congress to admit refugee children outside the quota was defeated. Children's organizations slaved heroically to bring out Jewish children from Germany, and they had some success: more than five thousand went to Palestine, and the children's transports organized by the British saved more than eight thousand of these youngsters, several of them our cherished friends today. But for more adequate numbers the world, still in the grip of the Great Depression and suffering large-scale unemployment, coupled in all too many places with a reluctance to add Jews to their mix of population, offered no haven. It was as though the detailed, heart-rending, and infuriating stories in the *New York Times* or the *Manchester Guardian* were just tales from a faraway land.

Aware how little the world seemed to care but intent on not giving up, we waited for word from the consulates we had besieged; at the same time, we waited to hear from those who had been dragged to concentration camps the morning of November 10 to be blackmailed, bullied, starved, physically abused and in some places tortured. A few weeks later, most of these prisoners began to drift back home. Their path to deliverance was paved with the promise to emigrate expeditiously, to a guaranteed place of refuge; others were released because the commandant had decided, for whatever capricious reasons, to let them go. The camps were pigsties awash in disgraceful, often savage excesses consistent with the humiliation rituals started with Kristallnacht. The guards were arbitrary, harsh, often sadistic; they beat their prisoners, kept them freezing and hungry, commanded them to perform impossible tasks, and then punished those unable to carry them out. The emphasis was on filth: inmates had trouble finding water to clean themselves, and many of them were compelled to stand in their own shit, a posture not only disgusting but unsafe; many inmates suffered from serious diarrhea. These were not extermination camps, but the guards exterminated a number even so. Suicide was a common way out for the captives. Some died; some went mad; more came back mental wrecks. All bore the stigma of being treated worse than animals.

One of the hapless victims of this beastliness was my friend Herr Schreiber, whom I happened to encounter in early December not far from our house. He had visibly aged, looked deathly pale, seemed disoriented, I thought almost senile. Our conversation was all too brief; it was almost as though he could not bear to talk to anyone, even me, at any length. He did tell me that he and his family would go to Shanghai, at that time literally the only place in the world that would admit immigrants without requiring papers or fees. Even this beckoning refuge, though, halfway across the world, was not open to everyone. The passage was out of reach for Jews whom the Third Reich had fleeced for years and further bankrupted by its post-Kristallnacht exactions. For too many German Jews, safety was a seductive mirage, ever receding the closer they thought they were approaching it.

The other graduate of a concentration camp I sa
those days was my Onkel Moritz Jaschkowitz, who can
through Berlin on his way home to Breslau. He had dropped
a great deal of weight, which made him look rather different—it almost suited him. But essentially he was the same
man; despite everything, his sense of the absurd was working
at full speed. I only wish I could recall our intimate conclave,
and I curse my partial amnesia. This much I see before me:
my father, my mother, and I are sitting in our peaceful,
brightly lit living room listening to Onkel Moritz. But all that
has stayed in my mind, and powerfully so, is that when he
told us about his four weeks at Sachsenhausen, we all
laughed heartily. It was a folly we three shared with him; a
conspiracy to laugh that we might not cry; a desperate and
for the moment successful effort to push away our terror. In
retrospect, it was a more shocking afternoon than one that
would have dwelt freely on Onkel Moritz's nightmare.

Other traumas awaited us. One scene from those days
remains anchored in my mind as though it had taken place
only a few hours ago. It is the twenty-fourth of December
1938. I am trying on a winter coat my parents had had custom
made for me, by far the most luxurious piece of clothing I
had ever owned, a solid dark gray wool with two rows of
substantial buttons, weighing on my shoulders with authority.
It is a coat for the English winter. Plainly, the notion of a
refuge in some subtropical land had not yet entered their
minds when they ordered it. As I stand there in my protective
shell, the bell rings; it is the mailman with a letter from the
British consulate. My heart beating, I watch my father open
it—a refusal to grant us permission to settle in Great Britain,
polite but final. I can reexperience my dismay even now as I
write; then I needed all my carefully cultivated self-control,
supported by my parents' presence, to keep from breaking
down at this latest blow. That the British Home Office was
inadvertently doing us a favor did not emerge for years. It
certainly did not seem like a favor in December 1938.

elf-discipline, I was discovering that this
ejections was having a noticeable effect on
bouts of depression, enough for me to notice.
iced it, too, and made me go to a doctor—a
of course. I explained my symptoms, especially
roubling me a great deal: I noticed that I was,
as it were, steadily watching myself, as though a double were
sitting on my shoulder and commenting on, or criticizing,
what I was saying or thinking or feeling. All spontaneity
seemed to have drained from me. The doctor listened sym-
pathetically and told me that I had an inferiority complex. I
had never heard of such an ailment and protested vigorously
that I did not feel inferior to anyone; my parents had taught
me that I was as good as anyone else, no matter what the
Nazi liars said. I did not convince him, but he gave me hope:
once I was out of the country, he thought, I would surely
feel better.

The United States, I need hardly repeat, was our ultimate
goal. But would we reach it in time? We did have the affidavit. The affidavit! How often did I hear that magical word
spoken with longing or with satisfaction during these months,
as German Jews frantic to get out did what my father was
doing: searching American telephone books for long-lost relatives or only for someone with a name that resembled their
own. The rule of thumb we all knew by heart was that the
better off the American signer of the affidavit, or the more
closely related to the petitioner, the more likely the American
authorities would judge it acceptable.

On that score we were most fortunate, but the misfortune
of my father's "Polishness" meant that we would probably
have to wait for years, far too long for sanity or even survival.
And after the British turned us down, we had only one scenario left: to secure asylum in the New World. I do not believe that we ever discussed the Shanghai option: the nearer
to our American relatives we could settle, the better it would

be. Our correspondence with Quincy, Florida, and the other Kwilecki headquarters, Bainbridge, Georgia, was far more frequent now; it remained businesslike but grew increasingly Aesopian. There was so much we wanted to say and to know, but both desires were largely frustrated by the feared blue pencil of the censor. Understatement was safer and in any event suited the style of Onkel Alfred and my parents. Thus short communiqués, dealing calmly with practical matters, crossed the Atlantic weekly and even more often.

We heard only later about the conversations that our American family—my Onkel Alfred, my Aunt Grace, and the rest of the Kwileckis—were carrying on at this time in our behalf with political acquaintances like Walter George, the influential senator from Georgia, and Edward Cox, the local congressman. (In thanks for their assistance, my uncles took their legislator friends deep-sea fishing—a typical American gesture, I thought when I learned of it.) Together they agreed that there was not a chance of putting our affidavit to use soon. Tante Hede, Onkel Samuel, and cousin Edgar, all on the German quota, might enter the United States some time before us. But they asserted that the United States was not about to modify its rigid quotas for my father's benefit.

A glance back at the American political climate at the time suggests that they were right. Too many forces were arrayed against opening the proverbial land of immigrants any wider. The position that President Roosevelt, whom we idolized, took on this sensitive issue was of necessity complex. He denounced Kristallnacht in a strongly worded statement on November 15; three days later he announced that he was taking advantage of a loophole to order an extension of the visitors' visas held by well over twelve thousand German refugees. But he announced that he would not ask for what he could not get. Public opinion was ill-informed, still strongly isolationist, only too indifferent to crises far away; and it was skeptical of horror stories, even true ones, reminiscent of the Allies' mendacious anti-German propaganda in the First

World War about Huns spearing Belgian babies on their bayonets. Noisy pro-Nazis had a certain, though a distinctly minor, following; far more dangerous to our future was the internal resistance of anti-Semites in high places. The most notorious of these was Breckenridge Long of the State Department, who sabotaged the entry of German Jews to the best of his ability. In a memorandum of 1940 he instructed consulates to "resort to various devices which would postpone and postpone the granting of the visas." In the light of such opposition, Onkel Alfred and his family would have to buy us asylum in one of the Latin American countries now trading visas for money. Their solution after shopping around was Cuba.

This was only a short first stage on the race to freedom. After Kristallnacht, the Nazis invented ever new sources of blackmail beyond that billion-mark "penalty," exactions that Jews had to meet before they could obtain a passport. Jewish families were obliged to surrender their jewelry, including their wedding rings, their silver, and other valuables. To turn the screws even more tightly, the regime ordained that while Jews were struggling to meet all these extortionate demands, they must show proof of admission to some other country—any other country—and of guaranteed passage. And in order to impose some semblance of order on the crush of German Jews trying to flee what was no longer their homeland, the Nazis decreed that potential emigrants must show a certificate of passage dated less than a month ahead before they could apply for a passport.

These shakedowns for a crime we had not committed roused my father's combative impulses to new heights. Before we could run the gantlet of officials who would at the end reward us with our ticket to freedom, he needed several signed pieces of paper proving that we had given up what the government had ordered us to give up. He procured them all by illegal and risky means. With Emil Busse's assistance, he made up a package, filled it with some heavy material, and turned it in at the post office, declaring it to be my mother's jewels and our silverware. I am not sure just how he managed to get a receipt that would be impossible to trace to him—I failed to ask him how he managed this feat, and by the early 1950s, when such matters began to interest me strongly, he was too ill to recall; nor could Busse, for all his splendid memory, reconstruct how my father made it happen. But he did make it happen, and how he did it remains one of the conundrums of my early life that I shall never solve.

This certificate was, of course, one of the critical documents we needed before we could subject ourselves to the bureaucrats holding us at ransom for our passports. My father somehow did not believe that he could smuggle our valuables abroad, and so, with full confidence, he turned my mother's rings and necklaces and our silver over to Busse. One can hardly ask a fifteen-year-old boy to pay attention to such trivia as his mother's jewels, but I had handled the silver often enough to remember it well. It was a plain, handsome pattern with narrow ornamentation around the edges, the knives, forks, and soup spoons unusually heavy, beautifully balanced, and a pleasure to handle, the coffee spoons and dessert forks in contrast small and delicate. I had no idea how much all this was worth, but it seemed to me that it must be valuable indeed.

Busse proved indispensable to us in another way. As my father's stamp collection had grown with the years, it had become a major piece of property containing some rare items. They would be permitted to leave the country only if their value did not exceed a certain set amount. Accordingly, taking Busse with him, my father visited a stamp dealer who was also a government functionary to have his collection appraised. As the dealer went through his task methodically item by item, noting down the totals and moving the stamps from one pile to another, my father, with Busse's connivance, kept him occupied with philatelic chatter; whenever the appraiser turned away to consult a specialized catalog, he shoved a few stamps from the first pile to the second. I have often wondered whether this dealer was lax, dimwitted, or decent at heart; in a country where arbitrariness is king, it was from such incidents that fortunes were made and lost, lives saved and doomed. Whatever the dealer's reasons, he seemed not to notice the irregular goings-on and certified my father's collection as not too valuable to be exported.

There remained the question of transporting it to the United States, where my father hoped it might serve as the foundation of our future prosperity (it did not). Having lost all faith that the Nazi authorities would respect arrangements already agreed upon and anxious lest his collection might be confiscated at the last moment by some capricious customs official, my father hit on an ingenious plan for getting his stamps to Quincy. It did justice to his sardonic sense of humor, which the past six years had not erased but had laced with bitterness. For many years he had been a moderate smoker, buying a brand made by Reemstma. To make their product even more appealing, the firm enclosed a coupon numbered from 1 to 50 in each box. Once a smoker had gathered a certain number of complete runs, he could order a handsome album from an array of offerings with ample commentary and empty squares into which pictures, supplied by Reemstma separately in neat packs, would fit.

Now, early in 1939, my father sent for such an album and chose a history of the Nazi Party, a volume that stank of self-satisfied and self-aggrandizing propaganda for the prehistory of the Third Reich. With grim satisfaction, he placed a stamp in the center of each square and pasted the photograph over it, carefully confining the glue to its four corners. He then mailed this hidden little fortune to my Onkel Alfred at ordinary book rate, only alerting him that a present from Germany would soon arrive. I still cherish the day in 1941 when my father and I opened this gift, which had arrived intact. We delicately peeled each photograph away to rescue the stamp underneath, and then threw the brown-covered album and the pictures of marching brownshirts and grinning Nazi thugs into the garbage.

My father grew even more daring and more high-handed as events around us seemed, he thought, to make extraordinary steps all the more necessary. On March 15, 1939, the Nazis had taken over the rest of Czechoslovakia, tearing up the Munich agreements in a predictable piece of treachery which profoundly humiliated the appeasers, who had thought that Hitler could be trusted or bought off with limited gains. I remember it well because on that day I became certain— and fearful—that this would mean war and strand us in Germany. It seemed to me inconceivable that the great Western powers would sit silently by as Nazi Germany consolidated its hold over central Europe. The British, far more than the French, started to talk tough, but there was no war. On March 19, Goebbels scornfully confided to his diary that Chamberlain had given a stern speech protesting the Germans' treaty breaking: "That's only hysterical screaming" after the fact, he wrote, "which leaves us completely cold." The sense of omnipotence that Munich had given the Nazi leadership had not faded.

Still, mounting international tensions only exacerbated our anxiety. The other Fröhlichs had already left for Cuba. Our turn was next; our visas to Cuba seemed to be in order and we had complied with exit regulations—in our own rather peculiar way. What remained was to find passage. With the help of my father's old friend Walther Kern, who had moved to Hamburg, the home base of the Hamburg-Amerika line, my father made what seemed like the best possible choice. He secured reservations on a large Hapag luxury liner, the *St. Louis*, which was due to sail to Havana on May 13. This meant that by mid-April we could apply for our passports.

It was now the end of March, only two weeks from holding that prize in our hands. But my father remained uneasy and would not be content with his arrangements. Whether he was making restitution for failing to organize our emigration in the early days of the Third Reich or feared that the regime might think up new torments for German Jews in the next few weeks, he resolved to hasten our departure no matter how hazardous the maneuvers this would force him to execute. Time was short. All we had was our tickets on the *St. Louis*. Aware of the gamble, yet persuaded that every day spent in Germany was a day of danger, he staked everything on booking earlier passage on another Hapag steamer. He found what he wanted in the *Iberia*, scheduled to sail on April 27, two weeks before the *St. Louis*.

Two weeks! It seemed like a very short time, but not to my father. Yet finding space for us on the *Iberia* was not enough: we still held our tickets on the *St. Louis*. There was no time to exchange documents. In this emergency, he decided to doctor our certificate of passage and substitute the new date and the name of the new ship for the old. The certificate looked and felt like a sham parchment printed in old-fashioned Gothic lettering. This was easier for a forger to work with than thin paper, but not really heavy enough to permit the clean rewriting he wanted. I can still see him at work committing this crime: using a straight razor, he gently scratched away at the ink, with *St. Louis* and *May 13* growing paler and paler. Little fragments of brownish paper pilled up under his fingers. To prevent the ink of his new entries from running, he smoothed with his thumbnail the surface he had roughened and with slow strokes, trying to imitate the bureaucratic handwriting he had erased, he inserted his substitutes. Had someone noticed, I think we would never have left the country alive, but no one questioned the document when we three confronted Nazi officialdom.

As my passport attests, our final appearance before the regime's emigration bureaucracy took place on April 7. The Nazis had appropriated a Jewish community center to serve as a collective bureau. We had to wend our way to a large

anteroom, where we stood crowded together with other sup-
plicants, as eager and as nervous as we were. Through an
open door we could see a grand office with a desk in the
middle and a self-important brownshirt sitting behind it.
More than once, as the crowd waiting to be admitted grew
too large to handle and a few persons standing at the front
were pushed into his sanctuary, he yelled at us to get back,
and all of us, intimidated and in no mood to argue, retreated
in haste. Cowed as we already were, these displays of inso-
lence, which could only cow us further, served just one purpose: to show off one man's power over the powerless. I
resented him beyond words, all the more because, however
strong my vengeful impulses, I was in no position to act on
them. My fantasies must have been lurid and bloody in the
extreme: my inability to feel rage, of which I have spoken,
never stopped me from hating the guts of the swine who were
lording it over us.

Once we got past this Aryan guardian into the open central space, as large as a ballroom, we saw desks all round its
periphery. We were told to stop at each of them to have yet
another form checked and stamped. The procedure took far
less time and proved far less exacting than we had feared; by
the end of the morning we were ready to go upstairs to an
office where our passports would be issued. But then perverse
nature threw an unforeseen hurdle into our path: my father
had a kidney-stone attack right in the building. This was not
the first time or the second; he had suffered from stones for
years. But it had never been so inconvenient as now.

My mother and I knew only too much about this excruciating affliction. During the years, my mother had learned
to administer shots, and we had a supply of morphine am-
pules at home, given us (illegally) by our physician, who
trusted my father not to become an addict. He was right:
fortunately for him, morphine slightly nauseated my father.
In any event, an attack, its course, and its alleviation were
all perfectly familiar to us. But now, on April 7, 1939? Did we

not have better things to do? I have never really wavered from my atheism, but it occurred to me that if there really was a god, he was showing his true colors—pure malice—that day.

We took a taxi home, my mother gave my father two shots just to be on the safe side, and we returned for our passports as though nothing had happened. It was a ludicrous episode, but whatever humor it contains emerged only in long retrospect. As the bureaucrat put the finishing touches on our documents while we sat across his desk waiting, my father, whom we had thoughtfully put between us, kept falling asleep. We would poke him gently and he would make an effort to stay awake, steadily lapsing back into his nap. But nothing went wrong, and we departed clutching our passports, conspicuously disfigured by the red *J* on the first page.

All that remained was to sell our belongings and pack a few of our things into whatever luggage we could manage to take along. I recall a standing suitcase, green with brass trimmings, a small edition of a steamer trunk. Accompanied by Onkel Siegfried, we took the train to Hamburg and boarded the *Iberia*. We left the country with the customary ten marks apiece (just $2.50 in those days) and, allowed to bring some personal property into our longed-for exile, with a small crate packed with whatever we prized most. This is the moment, I think, when my play and my novel were lost to posterity. We chose a handful of books, including the three-volume edition of plays by Curt Goetz (the inspiration for my comedy), and the tattered copy of Shaw's *St. Joan* somehow found its way into the crate, too.

More substantial was some fine china and crystal that my father had collected with his professional eye to high quality: a hand-painted china clock in dazzling cobalt blue as a present for my Aunt Grace, a splendid large crystal plate deeply and intricately incised, literally a masterpiece that an apprentice had carved as proof of his competence. Nowadays, Ruth and I bring out this wonder, at once a poignant reminder and an aesthetic delight, whenever we want a particularly handsome display for fruit on our dining table. One of our most remarkable possessions, a large, beautifully cut three-legged crystal bowl that my father had packed with his masterly expertise, was broken in transit; there was evidence that customs officials opened the crate and did not repack it properly. Fortunately, the photo album my mother had started for me and my father's sports photographs from his Frankfurt days were also rescued and resurfaced more than half a century later.

Just before we left I had another shock, very personal and, most people would say, trifling. Yet it remains among my memories and must have held some special meaning for me. Our buffet, the repository of my favorite secrets and my favorite food, my silent companion through the years, turned out to be less monumental than I had always imagined it to be. I learned to my dismay when the two men from the moving company quite unceremoniously lifted off the top and carried it out on its own that it was not a single, truly massive whole. I felt as though an old friend had betrayed me. Apparently nothing was stable or reliable in my world.

Our voyage on the *Iberia* was perfectly uneventful. The captain and the crew treated us not as undesirable inferiors being shipped off to tropical exile but as valued passengers. They even issued one of those festive little booklets listing the names of everyone aboard. We leaned back in our deck chairs like ordinary tourists, breathing in the bracing sea air, obediently drinking our bouillon when it was bouillon-drinking time, and taking naps in the sun. In my meticulous way I charted our progress by drawing a map recording our brief stays at Antwerp, Southampton, Cherbourg, and Lisbon, each passing day marked by a flag. I decorated the sheet with a photograph of the three of us on board and an inscription with a rather obvious pun on our name: *Dies ist eine unbestreitbar Fröhliche Familie*—This is indisputably a cheerful family. I remember only Lisbon, where we spent a day and enjoyed the Portuguese spring. The city was dressed in delicious foliage; the photos we took show us strolling about, but the hours on land swim together in my mind as green, more green, a sea of green. I had never seen so luxurious a display.

We did not exult. Trained to discretion, we kept quiet on that journey, mindful that we were still on German territory. We need not have worried; no one in the crew misbehaved. Then, finally, on May 13: Havana and freedom. On my map I drew a flag larger than the others, decorated with the laconic word *Ziel*—Goal. But even then I knew that my real goal was elsewhere: I drew an arrow northward, with the name *Quincy* followed by a question mark.

Then a final shock. As we debarked, I was overtaken by a powerful depression, one that I could not explain. It seemed for a moment as though I had never left Berlin. The vast physical distance from Nazi Germany, even the free air we had yearned so desperately to breathe, had not automatically diminished the pressure of the past, let alone erased it. The doctor's prediction that once I was out from under the Nazis I would be fine had been wrong, or at least hasty. In fact, much of Berlin, my poisoned source, would continue to hang over me like an sinister shadow—though less and less oppressively as the years went by. I made something of myself and have known happiness once again. But some sixty years later, fragments of Nazi Berlin still sometimes haunt me and will haunt me to the day I die.

NINE

A Long Silence

Try as I might to erase my six years under the Nazis from my mind—and I tried!—my past would not let me alone. The German-Jewish refugee community in Havana, numbering well over three thousand, clung together and talked Germany: who was still caught in the Nazi trap and what one could do to help. The latest news on the world stage added to our agitation. Even if the western European powers had shied away from a decisive confrontation in mid-March, when the Nazis took over all of Czechoslovakia, the high probability of war, half-desired and half-dreaded, was the topic of daily conversation; how many provocations would Britain and France swallow without more than impotent scolding? The question had deep personal meaning for us. War, apparently the only way of toppling Hitler and his gang, would close off all hope for flight to my father's brother Siege and his two sisters, Tante Esther and Tante Recha. And we had friends in Germany, Jewish and gentile alike, to worry over: the first desperate to find a refuge that would accept them, the second principled and often not very prudent anti-Nazis, in danger of landing in a concentration camp through some indiscretion.

Our ties to our former homeland, then, remained intimate and inescapable, a cause for wrenching anxieties. One other link, though, had a certain charm to it, the charm of revenge. It illustrates my father's ability to translate rage into action—a scheme I applauded enthusiastically. In March and April 1939, amid all our haste, all our time-consuming efforts to wrench ourselves free, my father had devoted precious hours to compiling a meticulous dossier on the income taxes the firm Fröhlich und Pelz had evaded through the years. It added up to a bulky document; once complete, he handed it over to Busse with instructions to mail it after enough time had elapsed for us to be safely out of reach. Sitting in Havana and thinking of the partner who had cheated my father in a time of stress, we gloated at the prospect of Pelz in jail. (We learned after the war that we had gloated in vain; at the last minute Busse, with good reason troubled that he might become uncomfortably involved in this affair, decided not to mail the denunciation.)

We settled down quickly. Our address: Calle 5, No. 89, entre 10 y 12, a nondescript house in Almendares, a run-down quarter. But there was no peace; just twelve days after we landed in Cuba, the tentacles of Hitler's Reich reached across the Atlantic to remind us of how narrow our escape had been. On May 27 the *St. Louis* steamed into Havana harbor. This, of course, was the ship on which we had held passage until my father had managed to move us to the *Iberia* and to forge the document that guaranteed our new reservations. The *St. Louis* had been making its leisurely way across the Atlantic with a few dozen genuine tourists and 907 German-Jewish refugees on board. Each of them had a landing permit bought from Cuban bureaucrats, the kind of legal bribe that our American family had bought for us. Then without warning the president of the country, Federico Laredo Bru, invalidated these permits. His action, wholly arbitrary, was a mixture of political gamesmanship and personal greed: a power play between himself and his chief rival, Fulgencio Batista, a craven response to xenophobic opinion on the island, and a design to enrich himself by selling what had already been sold once before.

Like nearly all other German refugees in Havana, we rushed to the harbor to stare at the *St. Louis* bobbing at anchor, almost close enough to be touched. I have in my possession Onkel Siegfried's laconic pocket diary for 1939; half of it left without an entry or the day dismissed with the phrase "nothing new." But, for all its lack of drama, it records that he, too, was among the spectators. "Went to the harbor," he noted on May 28, the second day of the tragedy playing itself out before our eyes. "*St. Louis* passengers still on board." Some of the more prosperous refugees—we were not among them—hired small boats that circled the ship and shouted encouragement. Jewish relief organizations sprang into action. They negotiated with the Cuban authorities, offered ransom to meet ever escalating demands, and were kept in suspense as hope and despair alternated from hour to hour. "*St. Louis* passengers still on board," Onkel Siegfried reported on May 29. Then, on June 2, the upshot: "*St. Louis* departed with 1,000 passengers for Santo Domingo."

Even after Cuban officials had announced their "final" decision, horse trading continued as the ship aimlessly cruised in Caribbean waters in hopes of a settlement. In the end, the waiting proved futile. After American authorities had energetically rejected a proposal to allow the *St. Louis* to dock in any U.S. harbor, the Dominican Republic seemed one possible resolution of the passengers' predicament. But these negotiations, too, failed, and the passengers faced being forcibly returned to Nazi Germany. The prospect of a concentration camp was as probable as it was intolerable.

It requires little imagination to reconstruct the mood of the refugees on the *St. Louis*. Several tried to commit suicide; others threatened to sabotage the vessel. The captain, Gustav Schroeder, a "good German" if there ever was one, kept in steady touch with the activist *Sabotagekomite* and tried to delay the return of the *St. Louis* to Hamburg as long as he humanly could. In concert with his subordinates, he even hatched a scheme to run the ship aground on England's southern coast. But that audacious move proved unnecessary as four countries—Britain, France, Belgium, and the Netherlands—each offered to take a quarter of the refugees. We followed the vertiginous oscillation of events with mingled anger and bitter disappointment. I found the refusal of the Americans to rescue a handful of pariahs in deadly danger particularly shameful. Almost from the beginning of my stay in the New World, my idealization of the United States had to endure some serious jolts.

For the 284 *St. Louis* passengers who landed in England, the country's humane action meant deliverance. For most of the others, their return would prove to be a death sentence: once German troops overran western Europe in May and June 1940, those who had been given shelter in Belgium, France, or the Netherlands were among the first Jews the victorious Nazis deported to the extermination camps. The balance sheet stands, and will forever stand, as a condemnation of greed, rigidity, and political cowardice; of the 623 refugees on the *St. Louis* given asylum on the Continent only about forty survived the war.

In the light of these events, my mother and I could only wonder at my father's brilliant prescience. My feelings resembled those I had harbored a decade earlier when he had bribed the doorman at the Scala to ask me whether I ate my meals. My father's authority was, if it had ever seemed in doubt, wholly vindicated. His determination, his courage, his prescience, his productive distrust of the arrangements he had first made, his good luck—the kind of luck that comes only to the deserving—call it what you will: it was thanks to him that we were looking at the *St. Louis* rather than traveling on it. Would I have survived if we too had been passengers on that ill-fated ship to end up an American citizen, an American family man, an American professor? The simple figures tell the story: the odds would have been against it.

Almost sixteen when we landed in Cuba and, as I have said, preternaturally serious, I was fully admitted to the refugees' apprehensive conversation. I find this somber figure hard to reconstruct now, for I think I have changed dramatically through the years. But photographs from that period and the comments of lifelong friends confirm my recollections. I was, an old friend recently told me, the palest person she had ever seen. I rarely laughed, rarely even smiled, and guarded my memories—my experience in the gymnasium, my working days as apprentice to a dental technician, my silent despair when I learned that Britain had refused us entry, Kristallnacht above all—as though they were secrets whose revelation would violate something that belonged to me alone. I could readily understand fellow refugees obsessively talking about their parents, their brothers and sisters and friends, still caught in that great prisonhouse called Germany. But this did not give anyone the right to pry into my life under Hitler.

My fixation on the future was perfectly understandable. I fully (and quite realistically) expected that sooner or later I would call the United States home, as did everyone else in our little group. Like the Jewish Eastern Europeans who in 1946 and 1947 had graduated from the displaced persons' camps to German cities they could only hate, we lived in Cuba, as the saying went, sitting on our suitcases. But my resolute looking ahead was also a way of fending off what I had left behind—and not left behind. Just as I kept others away from my memories, I did my utmost to keep myself, too, away from them.

Fortunately, I had Havana to entertain me. Much of the city, spotted with many-storied buildings of recent vintage, still had the charm of an old settlement. I wondered at both as I walked past, and never entered, the few dazzling hotels built mainly for American tourists or survivals from the time of Spanish rule. I enjoyed long strolls along the harbor and observed the fascinating exemplars of complex racial mixtures I encountered everywhere. The offspring of Spanish settlers, Central American Indians, blacks from the Caribbean islands, and Chinese immigrants had met and mingled here and—one can see that I referred almost everything back to Germany!—made for a colorful refutation of the Nazis' myth of "pure" stock. True, Cuban society had its own more or less subtle color hierarchies, but hardly anyone could convincingly sustain a claim to being a pure anything.

Havana, then, was the kind of city on which guidebooks like to bestow the all-purpose adjective *picturesque*. Vedado, the district where some of the more affluent refugees lived, was more pleasant for strolling than my own Almendares. What much intrigued me in Vedado was the coexistence of appalling slums with grand estates shielded from all disagreeable sights by forbidding walls. The very poor cheek by jowl with the very rich: I had never seen anything like it, and it awakened a political conscience that has stayed with me until today.

While we were glancing impatiently toward the American coast only a few dozen miles away, I picked up enough grocery-store Spanish to speak in my father's behalf to strolling hawkers of lottery tickets. They came in sheets of one hundred, and segments of them were fetchingly stuck into the vendors' hatbands. If one was content like my father to buy merely one or two shares, one could gamble with very little, and on occasion our lucky numbers brought us a few welcome pesetas. I also negotiated with the peasants who carried baskets of small, delicious, and very cheap pineapples: *Piñas*, they would shout, *piñas de la terra!* with that wonderful, lovingly prolonged, rolling *r* that few foreigners could ever hope to master.

Sugar was plentiful, so ice cream was exceedingly inexpensive, and, unrepentant chocoholic that I was, this matched my tastes to perfection. I liked to sit in Havana's ice cream parlors; they loom in my memory as spacious, pleasant, and cool caverns, with sleek, seemingly endless counters that could accommodate two dozen or more revolving stools. It was in these splendid establishments that I first glimpsed, and often tasted, specialties like sundaes or banana splits, delights unknown to me before. The baroque glass dishes in which these concoctions were served—fluted and elaborately curved—only intensified my pleasure; with an eye to the aesthetics of glassware, I was my father's son. I had to admit that the chocolate I consumed in large quantities did not match the quality of the confections my father had bought me in Berlin, but it would have to do—and did, quite well.

The transportation that brought us from the center of town to Almendares only underscored my newly found radicalism. Havana's buses were operated by drivers in rags who enjoyed nothing so much as running over a stray cat or dog, of which thousands roamed the streets. The mailmen were no less seedy and were as likely to steal a letter as to deliver it if they suspected that it might contain something of value. (My American family, quickly apprised of this unorthodox self-help, adjusted their mailings to us accordingly; they would enclose a single check or ten-dollar bill in a letter short enough to avoid arousing greed but opaque enough to conceal the money.) Among public servants, only the soldiers were well outfitted; they sported clean khakis, shined shoes, and neat caps and looked sleek, like walking advertisements for the blessings of good health and for privileged access to power.

I have said that fortunately Havana entertained me. Just as fortunately, nearly all the entertainment was free. We were exceedingly conscious of living off our openhanded American family. Though we did not stint ourselves so severely that we went hungry or bought second-hand clothes—Onkel Alfred or Aunt Grace would not have wanted that—we were only too aware that financial canniness was a most desirable trait in a refugee. Hence a central ingredient in our Spartan menus was the cheapest cut of meat available: oxtail. With its pungent flavor, it could serve as an ingredient in a hearty soup or as a dish on its own. We ate it very often, all too often: since leaving Cuba I have never been able to eat or even smell oxtail without an attack of nausea. At home in Berlin we had never been reduced to oxtail; after the limbo of Havana was behind us, it stood for me as a loathed reminder of poverty and dependence.

Our efforts at economy were all the more pressing because refugees were forbidden to work lest they take jobs a Cuban could have filled. Our conspicuous nonconsumption, then, was dictated by a sense of obligation and legal restrictions alike. Yet our abstinence had its limits. I remember my father buying me a white linen jacket: we did have money for that kind of necessity. For that jacket was, one might say, a cultural necessity: singed by the heat, we refugees would strip to our shirtsleeves only to be sniffily informed that in Cuba gentlemen wore coats and that we newcomers were guests who would do well to conform to our hosts' style of living.

Another necessity had a personal meaning for me: medical attention. I forget just how, but one day I broke my arm. I was in considerable distress, and my father rushed me to a clinic. There we found ourselves at the end of a long line, and so, to speed up access to a physician, my father bribed an attendant with a few pesetas. Almost instantly I was being attended to and free of pain. I need hardly note that this episode fostered my political education—what could be a more glaring illustration of the power of money?

True luxuries, though, were by definition beyond our ken, even if the boundaries between what we were entitled to and what we must forgo were somewhat fluid. I remember going to the Fausto, a cavernous movie theatre in the center of town; in this pleasure palace a ticket for a seat in the balcony,

a steeply pitched affair where you picked your way in almost
total darkness, must have cost very little. It was at the Fausto
that I saw *Gone with the Wind,* not without some twinges of
memory: how far I had come from the time, just two years
before, when I had read the novel—in Germany, in German.

It was my indulgence in a particular film (I have forgotten
which one) that greatly irritated my father: I had gone to an
expensive movie house, the forty-centavo kind. Surely fifteen-
centavo theatres could have served me just as well! I believe
this was the only time during our nearly two years in Havana
that my father grew angry at me. Perhaps that is why this
domestic storm, brief as it was, impressed me so much. I had
every reason to know my father to be a liberal man, but he
paused over every dollar he spent that he had not earned,
and he wanted me to be equally disciplined. After all, it had
been in order to husband "our" money that we had rented an
ordinary, sprawling one-story house in Almendares, which
easily accommodated eight or ten inhabitants. We had a good
front porch and a sizable living room, along with a number
of small bedrooms, an arrangement that made a little money
go a long way. Several distant cousins lived there along with
my parents and me. My mother, though, was forced to leave
it soon; her tuberculosis flared up, and she was condemned
to a sanatorium once again.

One incident I witnessed right at home was emblematic
of our predicament as refugees. One of our little tribe, Jacob
Wolfsohn, remotely related to us through Onkel Samuel's
side of the family, invented a powder designed to exterminate
cockroaches. In a country where the war against bugs of all
species was perpetually fought and invariably lost, where we
slept under mosquito netting in self-defense, and where some
types of roaches could fly, such a concoction could have
made its maker rich. In the experiments he performed on
our front porch, which I looked on with some suspense, the
results were unexpected: the roaches loved his stuff and
seemed to multiply at what seemed to us unprecedented

rates. Rather unfeelingly, we joked that his powder was an aphrodisiac. I must confess that we all found this fiasco rather entertaining; I may even have permitted myself a wry smile. But Jacob Wolfsohn's failure was not really very funny: it underscored our pathetic helplessness in a foreign clime after we had been robbed of our sustenance in Nazi Germany.

There was one thing, though, that we, especially the younger generation, could do without going into debt: we could spend a day at the beach with friends. It required only a bathing suit, a towel, and bus transportation, all of them affordable enough. This kind of excursion, though, had for the unwary expensive lessons of its own. It took me a while, and some drastic punishment, before I grasped that I was living in a subtropical climate: even hidden in the clouds, the insidious rays of the Cuban sun could do much damage to one's skin. I can still remember a spectacular sunburn after a day at the beach in March 1940—in March!—when the sky had been consistently overcast.

As the days and weeks went by in Havana, my highest priority was consistently to improve my English. A spot of good luck helped me along: I received a scholarship to the Havana Business Academy, a small school largely intended for Cubans preparing themselves for business dealings with Americans. There I learned how to write stilted business letters—"Yours of the 13th inst. received," and so forth. Typing was another essential skill. We were seated in front of office machines fairly antique even for 1939, while a phonograph emitted the rhythmic noises of a fashionable tune, the *Lambeth Walk*. To increase our typing speed, our teacher would replay the song at a faster and faster clip and thus at an increasingly higher pitch. The routine hurt my ears; I can still hum the melody, but, for the sake of my equanimity, prefer not to do so. In any event, I did learn to type fairly well. I also took a course in short-story composition. To my embarrassment, I recently found a folder marked "early writings," which included several typescripts, including sentimental love stories that I had perpetrated for that class.

All this was vaguely useful, but a highly popular class in English was far more profitable. It was run by a florid and ebullient Southern lady, I think from Atlanta, whom we knew only as Miss Jeannette. At the end of each class, she would present us with a new, preferably colloquial word. The only nugget I recall picking up this way—and there were many others—was *flabbergasted,* a word that I never use but sometimes think of with fond memories of Miss Jeannette. I should put on the record that, still signing myself Peter Fröhlich, it was while I was a pupil at the Havana Business Academy that I had my first publication. As editor of the mimeographed bilingual *Havana Business Herald,* an internal newsletter, decked out with a slick two-color cover, I wrote self-serving editorials praising the accomplishments of our school.

These achievements were reflected in my grades. I recently happened upon a report card from the Havana Business Academy for May and June 1940. On miserable grayish paper, it was the size of a postcard, a tribute to the amiable amateurishness of the place. Almost inescapably, it misspelled my name—I appeared as FROELICH—but the rest of the record was gratifying: nearly straight A's in the Short Story, Business Training, English, and Shorthand (a course I cannot remember ever taking). My Conduct and my Effort, too, were of A quality. The good boy had grown into the good adolescent.

My thoughtful Onkel Alfred further eased my progression toward command of English by buying us subscriptions to the *Saturday Evening Post, Collier's, Liberty,* and other magazines. This must have been a signal occasion for our small family: on June 6, three weeks after we had reached Havana, Onkel Siegfried noted in his diary that the first issue of *Time* had arrived and that a one-year subscription to *Life* was soon to start. It was from such fragments that the mosaic of my education was composed.

The American weeklies offered a varied fare, all of which I sampled, but I concentrated on the serialized novels; I would clip each installment and then swallow the whole, novels by now little regarded writers like Octavus Roy Cohen and Clarence Budington Kelland. *Time* magazine was another story. It was at the height of Timespeak, running words together *(cinemactress)*, inventing racy neologisms *(newshawk)*, characterizing people with two adjectives ("fortyish, balding"), and toying with the accepted word order of sentences ("cold ran the blood of the Finnish farmer," as Wolcott Gibbs memorably lampooned this distressing habit in *The New Yorker*). I do not think that these idiosyncrasies did my English permanent damage; by mid-1940, I had acquired enough proficiency to be amused by the verbal pirouettes that made *Time* unique.

Clearly I was on my way to mastery, increasingly able to follow news stories in Cuba's English-language daily, the *Havana Post,* which did not just report current events but prepared me for life in the United States. Its sports pages were particularly revealing and puzzling to me. America's national sport appeared to be something known as baseball, which, with its myriad rules and specialized vocabulary, I found hard to grasp. But just as I had done in Nazi Germany, in Havana I quickly became the fan of a team, the New York Yankees; though in 1940 they were not at the top of their form, sportswriters described the Yankees as laden with outstanding players. I learned quickly enough that to boast several batters with an average of above .300 and several pitchers who won twenty games a year was a rare good thing, and the Yankees had both. These were the winners with whom I cast my lot. Old habits die hard, I suppose, because they attest to permanent needs.

Some time in 1940 I scored a breakthrough, quite without my conscious assistance, that pleased me greatly: I started to dream in English. Other members of my family were far less at ease than I about acquiring a new language. Onkel Siegfried, for one, suffered with his lessons, though once in the United States his English became perfectly serviceable. He was forty-eight, a rather advanced age for a beginner. On June 26, 1939, a Monday, he reported the first lesson, and by the end of the week he had taken two more. But it was not easy for him; on July 3 he wrote in his terse way: "Today English lesson. Already the first difficulties." Those who condescend to German refugees might do well to ponder these homely efforts to make a new life under circumstances severe enough to paralyze most people.

I have said that refugees in Havana had one favorite topic: the prospects for their families still in Germany. As time went by, they added a second they canvassed no less obsessively: the List. For me this was easier to tolerate; at least it pointed forward to America rather than back to Germany. After the outbreak of war on September 1, 1939, with the German invasion of Poland, American consulates in Europe were closing, transferring batches of visas that had normally been their responsibility to consulates in countries untouched by war. By mid-September, Tante Hede and Edgar were on their way to the United States, and Onkel Samuel followed them some months later. When our names would appear on the List was not at all clear.

In Havana consular clerks did not summon individual families, but every few weeks they would post an array of names and invite thirty or forty families to present themselves to undergo the immigration ritual. Admission to the United States was not automatic, so the stakes could not be higher. Taking advantage of the tensions surrounding the List, a few refugees gained fleeting moments of fame by announcing with a knowing air just when the next one would be posted;

they knew someone who knew someone who was going out with a secretary at the consulate, and she had been asked to have a List ready for the coming Monday or Thursday. They were popular, these fortune tellers; our will to believe was too powerful for us not to grab at straws, even demonstrably fragile straws.

Unfortunately, sometimes weeks would go by and there was no List—certainly not for us. Then in January 1941 our time, too, came, but for my parents and me this long-awaited opportunity was as much a source of worry as of relief. My mother's tuberculosis was as active as ever; her stay in the sanatorium had not improved her condition. How was she to get through the compulsory medical examination? Tuberculosis, an extremely contagious disease, was a ground for exclusion, and consular physicians had been emphatically alerted to it. I knew from my frequent visits to my mother that TB is easy to detect; the tubercular cough alone, dry, short, and distinct from other coughs, is a telltale sign.

What could we do except appear at the consulate with my mother? If my father or I had ever been inclined to pray, we would have prayed at that moment. Instead, we consulted the physician in charge of her, and he gave her shots designed to simulate well-being, while she for once rouged her cheeks until she looked blooming, at least to a casual observer. A physician equipped with a stethoscope, though, is not a casual observer. Resigned to the ordeal to come, we appeared at the consulate. The doctor examined us three and passed my mother without a word. He made me think of the Berlin stamp dealer who had allowed my father's fine collection to leave the country. Was this doctor one of those burnt-out, drink-sodden exiles from Europe who populate some of Graham Greene's novels? Or was he an avuncular benefactor unwilling to split up a family? It is one of those mysteries in my life that I shall never unravel. Whatever the truth, my mother got her visa the same day my father and I got ours.

The last hurdle to our entering the United States had been cleared.

Our visas were valid for four months, and my mother's physician recommended that she remain in Cuba with my father until the early spring so that she would not be exposed to the rigors of an American winter. He further suggested that we find a sanatorium to which she could go without delay. We followed his advice; Onkel Alfred made the arrangements, and once my parents arrived in the United States in April, and after a round of family visits, she occupied a bed in the National Jewish Hospital in Denver. In those days before smog, when haze meant haze, Denver was a city thought to be beneficial to patients with lung trouble. As a matter of course we would go with her.

This issue settled, I had nothing to hold me in Cuba. Tante Hede and Onkel Samuel, supported by a munificent loan from our American family, had opened a small store in Atlanta much like the one in Berlin vandalized during Kristallnacht, and I could live with them behind the store until my parents arrived. Counting from the summer of 1937, when we made our first plans to emigrate, to my landing in the United States, my odyssey had taken four and a half years. On January 10, 1941, I stepped on American soil for the first time, at Key West. Berlin seemed far away, but that was an illusion; for years I would pick fragments of it from my skin as though I had wallowed among shards of broken glass.

My first years in the United States were full of incident and shaped my life in unexpected ways. Because the principal aim of this memoir is to track down the impact on me of Berlin in Nazi hands, I want to dwell on this phase of acclimatization mainly as it throws light on the more distant past. I can say categorically, though, that this time markedly lightened my burdens precisely with its accumulation of mundane detail: schooling, working, making friends. In 1976 I wrote a sketchy autobiographical essay titled "At Home in America"; the title was accurate enough—by then I had felt at home in America for some thirty-five years. Far more rapidly and far more thoroughly than I had thought possible, America had done its best to make me feel that I belonged. But this did not tempt me to break my self-imposed silence. There was no need to talk about my prison time in the Nazi Reich to my family, who, of course, knew all about it. So did other refugees. And I thought that the strangers I met, some of whom became good friends, could do without the dubious entertainment of anecdotes about my troubled history.

Such at least were my rationalizations. It did not occur to me then that I was hugging my past to my chest for intimate and irrational reasons of my own. I was cultivating a masochistic preoccupation with, even some pleasure in, my preponderantly melancholy mood. Not that I made a secret of the Jewishness the Nazis had imposed on me or my country of origin or the reasons for my flight. But my overriding desire was to become a good American. Shortly after he landed in the United States in late 1938, my cousin Hanns had changed his first name to Jack and translated his family name to Gay. Americans, he discovered, found Fröhlich hard to spell and impossible to pronounce. And Hanns—or, rather, Jack—wanted to say farewell, as categorically as he could, to the country of his birth in behalf of the country of his future. We applauded and imitated his decision: my father, Moritz, became Morris; I translated my middle name, Joachim, to Jack, and all three of us adopted my cousin's choice for a family name. I became Peter Gay.

Much that my father and I did during our American apprenticeship, then, we did with a glance back at the regime that had nearly murdered us. In May 1941, almost as soon as we had settled in Denver, we applied for citizenship, a gesture as anti-German as it was pro-American, an emblem of rage and of hope alike. We were in earnest and wanted to cut yet another tie to Germany, as drastically and as expeditiously as possible. My father and I moved into a very small, not unpleasant apartment, only a short bus ride away from my mother's hospital, so that we could visit her every day with ease. Our first, and for a long time our only, luxury was a portable phonograph for which we collected some of our favorite classics—with deliberate speed; our poverty made us all the more selective about the records we bought.

More important, we had to think about my education. After negotiations to disentangle my rather scattered schooling on two continents, I was admitted to East High School for the fall as a senior who would need to take only two courses to graduate with the class of 1942. My Americanization was moving forward at a rapid pace. Much to my father's astonishment and gentle disapproval, I made it all the more conspicuous by a passion for popular music, which I had acquired by listening to the radio in Cuba and now could indulge more freely. Try as he might, he could never appreciate my newfound enthusiasms: Glenn Miller and Artie Shaw. But to me, much as I enjoyed them for their own sake, they were a kind of statement, ingredients in my new identity.

To be sure, there were some connections with Germany that we could not and did not want to sever. There was no way of getting mail from Tante Esther or from Emil Busse. But we had one resource for finding out whatever could be found out: we subscribed to the *Aufbau,* the bible for all refugees from Germany, founded in 1934 as a monthly newsletter by a German-Jewish club in New York City. The growing isolation of Jews in Germany gave the *Aufbau* a new reason for existence. It became a bearer of important news to its anxious and desperately loyal clientele. In April 1939 the brilliant journalist Manfred George was appointed editor in chief, and half a year later, three weeks after Kristallnacht, he converted the *Aufbau* into a weekly. There was, from then on, more news than he could handle.

George mobilized an outstanding group of contributors, and the *Aufbau* featured articles on politics and on literature of absorbing interest to German Jews now in the United States; later it published indispensable lists of Jews missing and, less frequently, of Jews found in war-ravaged Europe. Thus the *Aufbau,* the lifeline of German Jews all over the world, was responsible for bringing together more German-Jewish families than anyone else anywhere. My father read it, as did virtually all refugees, from cover to cover.

I had other hints, less consequential than the pages of the *Aufbau* but scarcely less poignant, that I could not simply dismiss my past. One telling incident has stayed with me through all these years. I was immensely fortunate in my two teachers at East High: George Cavanaugh and Helen Hunter. Cavanaugh, who taught civics, took an interest in me and recommended reading fare uncommon for a high school student, especially a recent arrival—books like Thurman Arnold's sardonic dissection of America during the Depression, *The Folklore of Capitalism.* (I still have a copy of it, signed by its author to "Peter Gray," when Arnold was in Denver for a talk.) Miss Hunter, who taught us English, was quite as supportive and, as will emerge, even more influential in my life than Cavanaugh.

It was in one of her classes that the incident I mean took place: it made plain that the gulf between me and "real" Americans still yawned wide. Our assignment was to read and discuss a long epistolary story by Kressmann Taylor, "Address Unknown," published in 1938. At the time, it was extravagantly praised; Whit Burnett, editor of *Story* magazine, where it first appeared, called it "perfect." The protagonist is Max Eisenstein, an art dealer of German-Jewish origins resident in San Francisco. In the opening, stage-setting letter to his German friend and partner Martin Schulse, he voices unfading nostalgia for his faraway fatherland, its scenery and its food. Schulse, who has returned to Munich late in 1932, has been something of a political liberal, but as the Nazis take power, he quickly grows enamored of their ideology and tries to discontinue his correspondence with Eisenstein. Yet Eisenstein continues to write, begging his old friend to protect his gifted and beautiful younger sister, Griselle, an actress whom Schulse had once loved and professes to love still. Too brave and heedless to flinch from danger, she has left Vienna, where she is still safe, to open in a new play in Berlin. Eisenstein is worried for her: one of his letters to her has been returned with the ominous notation "addressee unknown."

Actually she is still alive, but she has been denounced and is about to be arrested. In flight, she turns up at Schulse's door pursued by brownshirts, but he turns her away. In a highly offensive letter—"A new Germany is being shaped here. We will soon show the world great things under our Glorious Leader"—he informs her brother that she was killed not far from his house and that he had heard her screams until she fell silent. Maddened by his former friend's callousness, Eisenstein resolves to avenge her. He sends Schulse letters that must appear suspicious to the most obtuse of censors. He writes darkly of having shipped "11 Picasso reproductions, 20 by 90, to branch galleries," messages that sound like coded, subversive communiqués. After receiving two or three such missives, Schulse pleads with Eisenstein to stop sending them; they have already seriously compromised him and his family, and worse is sure to follow. But the bereaved, unforgiving brother does not let up until one of his letters to Schulse is returned with a crisp message stamped on the envelope: *Adressat unbekannt*—addressee unknown.

The question before the class was not a literary but a moral one: was Eisenstein right to act as he did? The overwhelming majority of my classmates were inclined to blame him for his vindictiveness. What could Schulse have done, his house apparently full of family, a physician attending his ailing wife, a gang of Nazi thugs hot on Griselle's trail? He was on his way to becoming an outcast in his society; to aid a Jew, especially a hunted Jew, would have ruined whatever reputation he had left. I strongly dissented from this generous reading: *of course* the brother had been in the right! From this distance I can no longer reproduce my reasoning, but my quite unambiguous feelings remain in my mind: nothing bad that happened to a German, especially this kind of German but in effect any German, deserved to be criticized. I did not bother to justify my verdict by retailing stories about my years under the Nazis. My attitude was the triumph of experience over charity; it reminded me, if reminder was needed, that, unlike my classmates, likable innocents all, I was still entangled with my past.

All through the war my hatred of Germany and Germans retained this high pitch. I valued my rigidity and explained it to myself as consistency, as a simple, obvious, justifiable response to Nazi barbarism. I welcomed the Allied bombings of Hamburg and Cologne and any other city in Germany. Not even the massive air strike on Dresden, or for that matter on my "hometown," Berlin, troubled me in the least. Had the Germans not killed, wholesale, wherever they had gone? Had they not wantonly reduced the city of Rotterdam and the cathedral at Coventry to rubble? Had their judges not cynically sanctioned the assaults on Jews after Kristallnacht and looked the other way as concentration camp guards murdered inmates? Had the regime not given career criminals free run of the country? Were they not themselves the most vicious and most brazen of criminals? Had they not ruined the lives of millions of Jews in Germany and the rest of Europe? Had they not, as we then believed, killed thousands of them? During the war, of course, we did not know just how appalling their record of mass murder really was, but what we did know was bad enough to ratify my conviction that Eisenstein had acted properly.

I also had a strategic reason for my spiteful attitude. I was convinced that only the most sustained and most drastic action against the German hordes, the sworn enemies of civilization, could win the war. Years later, talking over these years with Busse, I heard with interest that he had welcomed every air raid on German soil, whether his life was endangered or not. Because his countrymen appeared unable and unwilling to free themselves of Hitler on their own, the British, the French, the Americans, and the Russians would have to do it for them. I had fully shared this kind of reasoning, but for me news of air raids on Germany was more than just a welcome indication that the Allies were determined to carry through the fight to the end. It was also satisfying an appetite, my imperious hankering for revenge.

When the Japanese struck at Pearl Harbor, I was a student at East High; the following day, along with the teachers and my schoolmates in the assembly hall, I heard President Roosevelt address the nation, defining December 7, 1941, for us as a day that would live in infamy. I could hardly help drawing a contrast between this solemn moment in which I was included without a moment's hesitation and the celebrations of some Nazi triumph in my Goethe Gymnasium, from which I had been expressly excluded. But the end of my student days was near; in January 1942 I had to drop out and take a job to help my father free us from further need for financial support.

My first job was as a shipping clerk in the Imperial Cap Factory, which employed some forty workers and produced nothing but army caps. At a time of frantic rearmament, all salesmanship was superfluous; orders flooded in from army bases all across the country. The establishment was owned and run by a Christian Scientist named Epstein, a slender man with a natty mustache who steadily chewed on a cigar and was plagued by a nervous cough. All day long I stood at my table listening to baseball broadcasts and packing the orders one after the other. My salary: all of $12 a week, which was raised to $16 when the minimum wage was raised to 40 cents an hour. When Mr. Epstein recognized that I was not cut out to be a lowly packer, he took me into his office to help with filing and correspondence. My teachers at the Havana Business Academy would have been proud of me.

Meanwhile my father's career as a salesman for manufacturers of sports coats and leisure jackets proved only indifferently successful, certainly at first. Traveling across Colorado in his little black second-hand Ford, he gallantly tried, struggling to improve his fragmentary English in night school, an experiment in Denver's adult education almost poetically called "Opportunity School." But the opportunities he created for himself were never quite enough. He did his best, but, in a slow and insidious way, Hitler had broken him. Whatever brave face he put on, however energetically he refused to be called a survivor (a badge of honor, he thought, that belonged only to those who had suffered in the camps), he too was a victim. When he died on January 18, 1955, the cause of death was called hardening of the arteries. But it is not sentimental to say that he died of a broken heart.

Late in 1942, reluctantly acknowledging his inability to make a satisfactory living as a traveling salesman, my father joined me in the Imperial Cap Factory to run the giant semiautomatic steam presses that cut the material for the caps. This was a taxing job in more ways than one; the operator had to maneuver the sharp-edged forms that cut through several layers of felt in such a way that as little of the expensive stuff as possible would be wasted. And it was physically strenuous, too, at least for my father, who was nearly fifty; he found pulling down the levers every few minutes almost beyond his powers. He had been sturdy enough all his life to carry packed suitcases, but this labor proved an excruciating exertion. I saw him straining at a chore for which he was never made, standing at his press without a word of complaint, his only satisfaction that he was keeping his self-respect. As I visualize him now, I think of those who have nagged at German refugees for more years than I care to remember—"Why didn't you leave earlier?" and "Why didn't you realize that though you loved the Germans, the Germans didn't love you?"—and could cheerfully throttle them.

Then, in December 1942, luckily for me it turned out,

both my father and I were fired from Imperial Cap for supporting the drive of the unorganized workforce to unionize. Mr. Epstein accused me of disloyalty: had I not graduated from labor to management by being promoted to his tiny office staff? He was technically right, even if my weekly pay had risen to only $20 a week. But I saw no conflict of interests: I thought the workers were overworked and underpaid—what about my father?—and I thought it my political duty to support their campaign to improve their lot. This, too, became part of my American education. The job I found soon after, in early 1943, as a clerk in a wholesale distributor of magazines for Denver and the surrounding region, was better paid and less stressful.

Unemployed, my father turned to an idea he had first hatched in the mid-1930s: he would try to capitalize on his stamp collection by launching a dealership. The innocuous hobby to which my parents had introduced me in Berlin when I was around nine was to be enlisted in a far more urgent enterprise. I helped after work and spent untold hours in my father's venture from the beginning: I typed letters to dealers and collectors, pasted up booklets of selections to be sent out on approval, composed small advertisements to be carried by stamp journals, and assisted at the little mail auctions we conducted from home. And we did realize some returns on the investment my father had made in the last years of our life in Berlin. But our concerted effort failed; we had the requisite expertise but not the requisite capital. It sometimes occurred to me that if my father had insisted, our American family might have staked us as it had staked Tante Hede's store in Atlanta. But it was not in him to ask for such help. Had they not saved our lives?

None of these vicissitudes slowed down my Americanization. My erotic education, on the other hand, continued to be slow and beset with psychological obstructions. For a time in 1942 I went out with Mr. Epstein's daughter (now what

177

was her first name? Ruth?) and took this as another good instance of Americanism at work: the shipping clerk dating the boss's daughter! The social egalitarianism I thought typically American was not set aside in any way when she "betrayed" me with a soldier stationed at Lowry Field. I thought I could understand her giving me up. My desire for women was if anything more exigent than ever, but I found on my dates for a soda or at one of the amusement parks popular with the young crowd in Denver that I had somehow incorporated some of my mother's anxiety symptoms: a crippling feeling of nausea when sitting in a restaurant with my date, or at a theatre or a concert hall. Just thinking about going out could be agony for hours before I left home. These symptoms of a deep maladjustment took years to wane; it was as though I was finding my sexual needs too untamed to handle safely. My Cuban contretemps with the homosexual soldier did not improve my confidence, and so I continued to retain my virginity until well after my college years.

For all these setbacks, I experienced 1943 as a banner year. My mother came home from the National Jewish Hospital after a series of three operations. She had undergone a procedure called a thoracoplasty, in which parts of several ribs are removed to collapse the tubercular lung and thus halt the spread of the disease. Less invasive techniques had been tried on her and failed, and she bore permanent marks from the operations. But she was as well as someone like her could be until, in 1977, she died of something else.

With her return our family was complete once more, and we had to move into a somewhat larger apartment. We settled for a place that bespoke impecuniousness, with a moderate-sized living-dining room; a diminutive windowless corner curtained off from the rest of the apartment that served as my parents' bedroom, reminiscent of the space they had occupied in Schweidnitzerstrasse 5, only much smaller; a tiny

kitchen, though sizable enough to permit my mother to produce endless dishes of chocolate pudding for me; and an
open space between the kitchen and my parents' "bedroom"
large enough to hold a desk, a small bookcase, and a sofa
bed—my domain.

In the same year we changed our name in court. As I
have said, we had adopted the name Gay quite informally
after arriving in the United States, and we knew that upon
being sworn in as American citizens, a happy event due in
the late spring of 1946, we could choose whatever name we
pleased. But, typically for him, my father wanted the change
to be made as a matter of law. That meant petitioning a court
in Denver. He was already losing his hearing, which made
his English lessons all the harder for him, but a local lawyer
coached him on the appropriate answers to the judge's questions. Asked whether he had ever been a Communist, my
father answered truthfully, "no." Asked whether he had ever
considered overthrowing the government of the United
States, he answered, again truthfully, "no." Finally, when the
judge asked him if he planned to become a good citizen, my
father, not hearing the question and pleased by the reception
of his earlier replies, answered "no." His lawyer mumbled
something and the judge let the answer go by. Again someone
in a position of power had refused to use it against us. Decency, I thought, was still alive, and we were its privileged
beneficiaries.

My father did his best, in fact, to be a good citizen-to-be.
When he encountered complaining refugees, whom he dis-
dainfully called "the *Byunskis*," he was pitiless with them.
This unlovely epithet was loosely based on an invidious comparison popular with a number of German Jews who had not
adjusted to the United States: *Bei uns in Deutschland war
alles besser,* they would say, "At home in Germany everything
was better." Though not normally a preacher, my father
would give little sermons on the text of gratitude. Emigrés

ought to be glad to be alive and to have landed in the hospitable, democratic United States. I thought these attacks on unworthy nostalgia for a hellhole pure music.

Another event dating from 1943 cheered me immensely: in the summer I was granted a full scholarship to the University of Denver. This enabled me to quit my daytime job and become at long last—I was already twenty—what my parents had always hoped I would be: a college student. My father was back selling men's clothes and doing somewhat better, and it was understood that I would keep on working evenings and weekends to make up for the loss of my income. I sold neckties at Cottrell's, the Man's Store; ice cream at the Purity Creamery; and shoes in a shoe store. It was in the last of these that once again I was fired: I manned the cash register, but my boss was disappointed in my lack of initiative in selling his merchandise. Plainly, my mother's son, who, she thought, should become another Walter Lippmann, was not likely to be at ease in the commercial world in which her family had always worked.

This, a few highlights apart, is not the place to explore my history as an undergraduate at the University of Denver in anecdotal detail. That it was a supreme opportunity for me to advance my education as an American is too obvious to require detailed commentary. There is one stroke of good fortune that allowed me to be admitted to D.U. and that I dare not omit. It is only one episode among many that permitted me to feel I belonged in my new country so thoroughly and so quickly, but none was more moving than this. One day in the spring of 1942, while I was busy packing caps for Mr. Epstein, an elderly lady with a limp whom my mother had never seen before came to visit her in the National Jewish Hospital. She introduced herself as Helen Hunter, my former teacher, and told my mother that it would be a shame if someone so gifted as I did not graduate from high school.

Some day I might want to go to college, and then where would I be?

She added that she had worked out a plan to which the principal of East High had assented: she would give me a private seminar which, if I did well in it, should suffice for graduation. I went to see her several times, and she assigned me papers on Shakespeare. The one I recall most clearly was based on the question, Was Hamlet mad? I knew nothing about Freud at the time or the diagnostic term *neurosis,* an intermediate state between madness and sanity. My conclusion, firmly based on Hamlet's self-description: he was a deeply troubled young man with sufficient reasons for his depression and miming of madness, but in perfect control of his mental faculties. This was good enough for Miss Hunter, and I graduated with the class of 1942, in absentia.

The atmosphere on campus on the part of professors and fellow students alike was even more cordial than I had dared to hope for. Still, I kept up my silence about my years under the Nazis some time longer, even with my new friends, and refused to take advantage of my German in choosing topics for term papers. Instead, I went far afield, exercising my pleasure in playful alliteration in a paper titled "Persia, Pawn of the Powers," in which I explored the dependency of what is now Iran on the great imperialist nations before the First World War. And in a paper on a deservedly obscure Spanish theorist defending Franco and Fascism, I put to use whatever Spanish I had retained in my headlong rush to speak American English.

As so often, though, my German past surprised me with its tenacity. One day after a class on the history of political thought conducted by one of my favorite professors, Dr. Pollard, I got into a good-natured but earnest discussion with him. The issue was the right of genius to transgress boundaries of taste and ethics. I gave Wagner as an instance of a major cultural figure whose anti-Semitism was unforgivable no matter how splendid his music. Pollard, a gentle man who mumbled more than he spoke, chose to disagree; a genius, he argued, is entitled to complete freedom from the limitations that hem in lesser men.

My English had made great strides in the two and a half years between landing on American soil and entering D.U. And one day during my freshman year, I had a golden opportunity to demonstrate that my studies were paying off handsomely and that I was secure in my English. I took a required speech course in which every student had to present a short talk in front of the class. Midway through my turn, Dr. Paul, a small-time Professor 'iggins, interrupted me and said, "Wait, you're not American-born, are you?" I allowed that I was not. "Let me guess," he said, and guessed, poor fellow, southern England, where I had never been.

Then, in the summer of 1945, I ended my silence. It was as though I had unconsciously waited for the right time, the right place, and the right company. My record at D.U. was unblemished, and my straight A's brought me another scholarship, this time to an international summer seminar at Salisbury in the hills of northwestern Connecticut, an earthly paradise. The Institute of World Affairs, which had been held there for more than twenty years, had been founded and was funded by a severe, old-fashioned, white-haired philanthropist named Maude Miner Hadden, who attended many of our sessions. We made ungrateful fun of her when she was not around, partly I think because we were a little afraid of her. Her idealism was straightforward and her means of translating it into reality was, I must say, to the point: to bring together for six weeks around thirty college students from all over the world—our class added up to thirty-six altogether—have them break up into workshops, and, as a group, listen to invited speakers, for the most part political scientists with a specialty in international relations.

We had a great deal to talk about. The war in Europe had

ended in early May, the war in Asia continued to drag on, and an American invasion of Japan, though everyone feared that it would be expensive in lives, was in prospect. But while we were at Salisbury the Americans dropped the atomic bomb on Hiroshima—for two days, I wrote at the time, we talked of nothing else—and Japanese resistance finally collapsed. Meanwhile, the United Nations, designed to avoid the fatal mistakes of the League of Nations, was being organized, and its chances for survival and possible handicaps made for lively, and, with one or two of our visitors, contentious talk.

The summer, with our indefatigable canvasses of the changing world around us and the intimacy in which we lived, also made for friendships, some of them lasting. With me, it even made for love. She was an enchanting, petite, and energetic beauty from Colby College in Maine, everyone's favorite for her consistent good spirits, gift for even-handed companionship, and untrammeled intelligence. It did not take me long to catch on that she did not feel about me as I felt about her, but this did not thwart our friendship.

My fellows found me excessively solemn and said so openly, I think affectionately; evidently I had not yet expelled the Nazi poison. But during discussions among ourselves or with visiting lecturers I gained a certain authority. I never hesitated to ask questions and managed to sweeten the sting of my criticisms with a tentative posture. The polite and non-committal phrase "I am wondering," my favorite gambit, became almost proverbial in our camp for a technique in which a velvet glove concealed, well, my iron fist.

On our hill in Salisbury we were far from civilization and so we made our own. Gasoline, still rationed, was short, which banished any thought of more than one or two collective excursions. But we invented what we considered to be a superior substitute: the leader of our seminar, Joseph Bailey, a vigorous, immensely likable member of the education faculty at Harvard, read to us in the evenings. His choice was Mark Twain's *The Mysterious Stranger,* the tale of a devil who visits the earth and finds humans deeply disillusioning. None of us had read the book, all of us were enthralled by it, and Uncle Joe (as we called him), obviously an experienced reader, would stop at a tense moment and send us off to bed with the announcement that the next installment would follow the next evening.

Another self-started entertainment that summer was an occasional forum led by some of us. And around halfway through our stay, three refugees from Hitler—from Austria, from Luxemburg, and from Germany—presented an evening of reminiscences. It was in this congenial atmosphere, seven years after the event, that I spoke of Kristallnacht for the first time and in graphic detail. The setting was perfect: surrounded by fellow students of whom I had grown fond, young men and women knowledgeable about the world in which I had grown up, I spoke freely. It was a memorable act of self-liberation.

It must have been more taxing and its effect on me more visible than I realized: after the session was over, my friend from Colby took me for a long walk in the moonlit countryside and talked nonsense at me to bring me back to earth. It was a helpful, characteristically generous gesture, and I was grateful. But what mattered to me most that day was that I had broken a long silence. It was as though a forbidding dam had finally burst, and now I might be free to rethink my feelings about my German past.

TEN

On Good Behavior

The year 1945 brought both peace and horror, greater horror even than before. By the time I had broken my silence, in midsummer, word of the death camps and the Nazis' murders of millions had trickled out of Europe. The Allied troops who liberated the camps in the west and their Russian partners who overran Auschwitz found shallow mass graves, piles of unburied bodies, collections of shoes and suitcases, and, perhaps more appalling still, living skeletons by the thousands. We were to learn—and some of this information took months, even years, to emerge—that the Nazis had continued their killing sprees to the end, even when they knew the war was irretrievably lost. After they were compelled to abandon their gas chambers in Poland, they had marched their starved and exhausted victims to death when they did not simply shoot them. And some of the murderers had killed with clinical detachment, in the service, they said, of science.

A tragically large number of the survivors did not long enjoy freedom and professional care. They died of the camps: of malnutrition, typhus, beatings, mortal indifference to their human dignity, loss of the sheer will to live. Some well-known survivors of Auschwitz would commit suicide many years after, unable to eradicate their despair despite the loves they inspired and the careers they forged. It was as though the bestiality they had suffered made this world an unfit place to live in. In the graphic words of Jean Améry, a survivor of Auschwitz who killed himself, the camps were *anus mundi,* the asshole of the world. The photographers and filmmakers who accompanied the conquering Allied armies put some of this inferno on the permanent record; seasoned soldiers, hardened by years of combat and ostensibly immune to surprise, were overcome by what they saw.

One only too typical exhibit was the slave labor camp of Ohrdruf, not far from Buchenwald, liberated by George Patton's divisions on April 4. It was for Patton the first of what he called the "horror camps." He particularly noted the diabolical ingenuity of the torture instruments designed to make the victim suffer as much as possible. The beating tables were designed to inflict the maximum pain without killing the captive, at least not promptly. Even those hanged at Ohrdruf— there seem to have been about four thousand of them in the first months of 1945—were suspended so that their death would be slow to come; it could take as much as fifteen agonizing minutes. Patton applauded the suggestion of a fellow officer, General Walton Walker, that the place be shown in all its raw hideousness to the mayor of the town. The mayor came, as did his wife, and on the way home both committed suicide. There should have been more.

The reports grew more grisly month after month; reports virtually incredible yet well substantiated—Jews rounded up in Polish villages and exterminated after they had been forced to dig their own graves, gypsies and homosexuals sacrificed to the sick fantasy of racial purity, Russian prisoners of war gunned down in cold blood. It made things worse, if this were possible, that not all the barbarians were fanatical Nazi party members or professional criminals; among those who quite enjoyed participating in collective murder there were, in the words of the historian Christopher Browning, "ordinary men." Nor were the Germans the only savages: Austrians, Poles, Ukrainians, Lithuanians, Latvians, Croatians did more than their share in trying to cleanse the world of that vermin, the Jew, whom they envied and despised. The reports of deadly anti-Semitism among Eastern Europeans, I must say, hardly astonished us; Poles, after all, indulged in massive pogroms after the war, murdering Jews who had survived somehow and ventured back "home." But Germans? Even after what my parents and I had experienced down to 1939, we were shaken by the ample supply of homicidal sadists among them. We, the lucky ones who had escaped all this, did not want to believe it and did not want to hear about it, but in spite of our most elaborate defensive maneuvers we listened.

Much of this record was enriched and elaborated to the world in the war crimes trials of Nürnberg, launched soon after the surrender of the Germans. Some of the verdicts were hard to understand: Franz von Papen, who more than any politician in the dying Weimar Republic had maneuvered Hitler into power, was acquitted. Others received more appropriate sentences; Göring cheated the executioner by taking poison, but Joachim von Ribbentrop, the former champagne salesman risen to foreign minister; Field Marshal Wilhelm Keitel, Hitler's man in the armed forces; Alfred Rosenberg, the party's most influential racial theorist; Hans Frank, who governed occupied Poland with exemplary brutality; Wilhelm Frick, one of Hitler's most devoted supporters and, as minister of the interior, responsible for enforcing the racial laws; Arthur Seyss-Inquart, the Austrian Nazi who managed his country's Anschluss to Germany and distinguished himself in his own way as governor of the occupied Netherlands; Ernst Kaltenbrunner, another Austrian who rose to high posts in "internal security"; General Alfred Jodl, one of Hitler's closest advisers; Fritz Sauckel, who after a long career in the party was responsible for slave labor; and last but by no means least, Julius Streicher—I have mentioned him before but I don't mind mentioning him again in this context—were hanged. All this gave me much satisfaction then, as it gives me satisfaction now to type these names.

I visualized, and visualize, the noose tightening, tightening. Other leading Nazis were condemned to death in later trials, and the Russians, with few legal scruples to delay them, proved exceptionally efficient if not always very discriminating.

It would be unjust to carnivores to bestow the label of "wild animal" on the Nazi leadership and the masses of militant followers who tried to make the Nazi New Order a reality; animals kill from instinct and hunger and have not had the advantage of studying Kant or learning the catechism. The abysses of human nature revealed in the Holocaust might even have given Freud pause. It was aggression at its ugliest and most unchecked, linked to a rush of power and, more perversely, in many killers to sexual excitement. When I reduced this monstrous catastrophe to the narrow world of my immediate family, as I did at times, the revelations made me shudder for my parents and me. We had almost been in it, too! I repeat what I said earlier: I refuse to call myself a survivor. But I still have moments when I think of my life as an astonishing gift.

The horror stories, all of them true, meant that we would almost certainly never see Tante Esther and Tante Recha again. Some time later—I do not remember when—we heard that Onkel Siege had survived the war; as the husband of a gentile woman who refused to divorce him, he was not arrested until January 1945 and escaped being transported to an extermination camp. More astonishing still, Onkel Moritz got through the war alive. On the way toward death in the east in one of those infamous cattle cars, he had jumped off the train and broken a leg; taken to a hospital, he seems to have gotten through the rest of war there. He was not sure just when they picked up Tante Esther, my lovely, melancholy, blonde aunt who had played Germania in school. Nor did he know where she was murdered.

He did have some information about Tante Recha that made her fate more infuriating than impenetrable ignorance would have been. Some time in 1941, when the Nazis still allowed a few Jews out of Greater Germany, she had a permit to enter England as a domestic servant, while her son, Michael, was scheduled to go to Palestine. But some bureaucratic muddle kept him from obtaining the papers he needed, and his mother decided to wait until the tangle had been straightened out. It was straightened out, but by that time her English permit had lapsed, and she became just another statistic, just another anonymous casualty of the Thousand Year Reich buried who knows where.

How did all this affect me? Any extensive comment would be superfluous and banal; I was, to put it tersely, enveloped in an aura of hatred and dismay. Hence my feeling at home in America, as it were authenticated by my new friends and my new intellectual environment, was all the more necessary to me: it seemed like a thrilling refutation of the view of human nature forced on me during my years in Nazi Berlin. For all my self-protective gestures, though, I did not refuse to talk about what had happened in the death camps. I even wrote about it. From the fall of 1944 until I graduated in early June 1946, I wrote a column on national and international politics for the *Denver Clarion*, my university's weekly newspaper. When Franklin Roosevelt died on April 12, 1945—when I came home from the university that afternoon, I found my mother weeping for him—I wrote the obituary for the *Clarion*. I seemed to the editors, and to myself, a natural choice.

I came upon some of my *Clarion* effusions recently—my mother's apprentice Walter Lippmann—and must admit that they were exceedingly earnest, even preachy, and excessively self-confident. I solved the world's problems each week in six hundred words. Looking back, I am amazed that the editors of the *Clarion* did not drop my column and that my fellow students never complained about it to me; perhaps they never bothered to read it. I titled it "The Gay Outlook"—I need hardly remind anyone that in those years such a title awakened no rich associations.

In any event, it was in a column of late November 1945 that I spoke feelingly about the "six million" Jews murdered by Hitler and of "the two million who remain alive," many "still vegetating in concentration camps." Even now, I added, "after liberation, thousands of Jews are committing suicide every month; they feel with deep bitterness that they are truly the forgotten people." Meanwhile, I charged, the world was showing a "cynical disregard" for the survivors' desperate plight. Surely the solution was to adopt President Truman's proposal to have Jews looking for a homeland admitted to Palestine. I was very severe with the obstructionists attempting to sidetrack this obvious and humane solution: the British policy makers who turned back ships laden with refugees had Jewish blood on their hands; the nationalistic Arabs who disregarded the wishes of their Palestinian brethren to bring in Jews who, after all, had "performed miracles"; and, ever evenhanded, the "rabid Zionists" who insisted on a purely Jewish state. Though I was not a Zionist, rabid or relaxed, I was willing to be rather indulgent about their terrorist acts, which I explained as an indication that "the Jews are getting fed up with the British double-dealing."

What strikes me about this column is how little I knew about the situation of Jews in Europe. This did not keep me from having strong feelings about them. I could have written some of that column today, especially about the "cynical disregard" of the world toward Jews, though I suppose I would now offer a more nuanced appraisal, being rather better informed than I was in 1945. But what most impresses me, despite all the changes that I would now make, is an essential continuity of attitudes. I had not forgotten the Americans who had refused asylum to the refugees on the *St. Louis,* and I have not forgotten it today. And if I was hard on the Allies, I was harder on the Germans.

This uncompromising rejection of my former fellow citizens followed me to Columbia University, where I registered in 1946 to study for my graduate degrees. In the first chapter of this memoir I talked about my undiminished anti-German frame of mind during these years, exhibited by my distaste for Franz Neumann's "sentimental" support of a Germany starting on the stony road to postwar democratic reconstruction. As I have said, graduate study compelled me to resume reading and doing research in German sources, something I had thought I would never do. In the end, even my doctoral dissertation, completed in 1951 and published as a book the following year, was on the German journalist and Social Democratic theorist Eduard Bernstein. But then, Bernstein had been an outsider to German society both as a Jew and as a Marxist. I did not know it then, but subtly and invisibly, I had taken a first step toward reconciliation.

I have already indicated more than once how steep my journey would be: I was near German soil in 1950, when I did research on Bernstein in Amsterdam at the International Institute for Social History. It would have taken little effort to visit my former fatherland, but I made no move. And in Amsterdam I heard a story that underscored my sense that Hitler had presided over a tribe of homicidal maniacs, as mad as they were murderous. The Institute, which occupied a spacious row house on the Keizersgracht, was seized by the Nazis in mid-May 1940, just after the German armies rushed through the Netherlands in a lightning campaign. The librarians were expelled, and Nazis took over. Once Amsterdam was liberated, the Dutch employees of the Institute rushed to their building and found it completely empty; even the tea service once in daily use was gone. Hoping against hope in chaotic postwar Europe, they advertised in socialist newspapers and periodicals and spread the word among booksellers. One day two Hamburg working men came upon an abandoned barge and boarded it to have their picnic. There they found wooden crates, carefully packed and nearly all of them untouched—the library of the Institute. In the midst of a great war, then, after the Allied invasion, when Nazi Germany was straining all its resources for its very survival, the fantastic program of establishing a vast museum—really, a mausoleum—displaying the range of international Jewry and of Marxism continued to have a high priority. No rational alibi can explain such insanity.

Accounts of this sort—the stream of news stories about victims and survivors, the Nürnberg trials—only sustained my resistance to a less emotional condemnation of Germany. In the years that followed, I watched postwar Germany with the hawk eyes of a diligent and vindictive probation officer. And I did not much like what I saw. Did Konrad Adenauer, chancellor of a country he was undertaking to ally with the democratic West, really need the services of Hans Globke, whose commentaries on the racist Nürnberg Laws had given him considerable notoriety, and who had served in the Ministry of the Interior to the end of the Nazi regime? Could the Berlin Philharmonic not find a conductor other than Herbert von Karajan, no doubt a mesmerizing musician but one who had joined the Nazi Party not once but twice?

Closer to home was my angry question, Did German universities have to continue employing professors who had made themselves cozily at home during Hitler's Reich? The adroitness of these chameleons was nothing short of amazing. Over the years I collected some savory instances, of which the literary historian Hermann August Korff was my favorite. His highly regarded and widely cited synthesis, the four-volume *Spirit of the Goethe Age,* published between 1927 and 1957, spanned the Nazi era. With his eye to facts, he dedicated the third volume, on early German romanticism, to *Den Helden unseres Freiheitskampfes*—The Heroes of Our Struggle for Freedom, and dated it *Leipzig, am Tage der Einnahme von Paris, 14. June 1940*—Leipzig, on the Day We Took Paris, June 14, 1940. But in 1949, when he reissued the volume virtually unchanged, he substituted a new dedication for the old by recalling his wife: *Der Unvergesslichen*—To the Unforgettable. And the date of the first edition now read sparsely, "Leipzig, June 1940."

Quite as repellent, though in a very different way, was the demeanor of guilt-ridden Germans toward the handful of Jews who had returned or the slightly larger handful who had survived the Nazis at home in hiding or passing. There were some fifteen thousand Jews in the country in 1945 compared with half a million in 1933, and gentile Germans treated them with a kind of greasy delicacy, an ostentatious admiration for everything that Jews said, did, or believed. With profound irony, its targets, sickened by this newfound love for Jews no matter how sincere, derided it as "white anti-Semitism."

No wonder, then, that my refusal to enter Germany during the 1950s, and the tenseness of my brief visit in 1961, which I have described in some detail, seemed understandable, almost inevitable. But gradually, not through some dramatic conversion but in a sequence of personal responses, I began to unfreeze a little. I cannot enumerate them all, but as significant moments in my life, three or four of them deserve notice here. The first, no doubt, was the reappearance of my parents' silverware, the valuable table service we had entrusted to Emil Busse. He had some difficulties tracking us down—we had changed not only our residence, after all, but also our name—but had held on to it faithfully through all the vicissitudes of war and shipped it to us as soon as he had found our address. My mother's jewelry, it turned out, had been stolen by a maid in his house, but what mattered was that he returned to us what he could so easily have kept for himself.

Here was a "good German," and his gesture brought back to mind his courageous loyalty to my father in the fall and winter of 1938. I had good evidence, too, among my father's papers, sparse as they were, that Busse was not alone. Among the few letters my father had providentially saved was one dated July 28, 1938, from the chief executive of a major supplier of glassware with whom he had done business for years. (The signature is an illegible scribble.) Evidently my father had notified the writer that he was planning to emigrate to the United States to build a new life. "All of us—*sämtliche unserer Herren*—enormously regret that you are leaving your firm and that conditions—*die Verhältnisse*—have forced this decision on you," ran his reply. "All of us enormously esteem your single-minded enterprise, sustained by your expert knowledge." He added, "We greatly regret that we will have to do without your enterprise in the future," and hoped that he would be able to discuss my father's plans in person at the next Leipzig fair. And he signed himself "with best regards."

Once fitted into the context of the time, this shows itself a remarkable document. It was mailed in late July 1938, after my father had been summarily dismissed from his firm and when the anti-Semitic policies of the government, even before Kristallnacht, made a declaration of undisguised affinity with a Jew unwelcome to the authorities, if not dangerous. To be sure, it displayed some of the prudence to which letter writers had become accustomed: it was "conditions," not Nazi persecutions, that were driving my father into emigration. Still, the writer left no doubt that he was speaking not just for himself but for the whole directorate. In looking forward to a private conversation at the next Leipzig fair, he showed himself as blind to the immediate future as my father; it was not just Jews who failed to predict the Nazis' speeding up of persecution. There was to be no more Leipzig fair for any Jew.

Yet however artless, the hope that he might talk privately with my father suggested that the writer expected to speak confidentially about matters that the boldest of letters could not safely contain. And the way he signed off was equally significant. In the Nazi Reich there were three kinds of closing formulas: "Heil Hitler" spoke of enthusiastic support for the regime and was obviously most highly favored; "Mit deutschem Gruss" expressed an allegiance to the Nazi system less feverish in tone though still within the circle of acceptability; but "best regards," an old-fashioned, intimate, nonideological phrase, was about as explicit a sign as a letter writer could give of his politically unreliable opinions.

That was not all. A few other letters in my father's possession dating from after the war attested that at least some of his old acquaintances from Eintracht Frankfurt still considered him their friend. One had spent years in the concentration camp at Dachau for making uncalled-for remarks after learning of his son's death at the front. Another, looking back cynically, told my father that "from 1939 on," though he was then already thirty-three years old, he "had to play soldier." My Onkel Siegfried, too, corresponded with old friends in Berlin. And so some broken ties were gradually being mended.

Then came *Wiedergutmachung*—restitution. Starting in 1952, the Adenauer government in West Germany undertook to contribute three billion marks to Israel and to add further millions of reparations to individual Jews who had claims against the Hitler regime for loss of properties, ruined businesses, broken careers. As I have noted, my father and mother did not object to these payments. For them they were not blood money but funds owed. "Peter," my mother wrote me in February 1958, "whenever we should get the money, we will be glad to take it." I must say that the pensions my parents received proved of considerable help to me; they reduced the burden of my contribution to their budget, which was becoming all the heavier as my father's health was declining and my mother could earn mere pennies stringing pearls for a local jeweler. In 1959 even I, after long bureaucratic wrangling, received some restitution. I was awarded five thousand marks for my interrupted and delayed education. I had not invented this claim: even though I doubled courses and completed my undergraduate work in three years, I was twenty-three before I got my bachelor's degree.

The public gestures and private testimonials of goodwill meant something to me, but they did not force me into a reappraisal. I was like a playwright with an idea for a historical-psychological drama who had already visualized several minor characters and one protagonist, Emil Busse, but who still needed a critical mass of dependable information and leading characters to share Busse's starring role to make the play work. If it were really true that, with our high moral aspirations, love of music and literature, and bourgeois capacity for hard and sustained work, we refugees had taken the true Germany with us, perhaps there were true Germans at home, too, not isolated martyrs but substantial numbers of citizens. The tragicomedy I envisaged must not remain the melodrama—good Germans abroad, bad Germans at home— by which I had lived for so long.

During the academic year 1963–64, much fell finally, rather fortuitously, into place. I was a fellow at the Center for Advanced Study in the Behavioral Sciences at Palo Alto and took my family—my wife and three stepdaughters—to a sunny stay in northern California. A collection of my essays on the French Enlightenment was soon to be published and I was planning to tackle a comprehensive interpretation of the Enlightenment not confined to France. There were six historians among the fellows, and they were stimulating company, not to forget the brilliant philosopher Carl "Peter" Hempel, whom I had come to know eight years before at Princeton, and who again proved a genial instructor in the logic of historical scholarship.

But it was the Brachers who supplied the needed complications that would let me break out of my fixed pattern of response to my native land. Karl Dietrich Bracher came to Palo Alto with an established reputation as an unsurpassed anatomist of the Nazis' way to power; his *Dissolution of the Weimar Republic* of 1955 and *The National-Socialist Seizure of Power* of 1960 had quickly become standard works. Justly so; they bear the mark of scrupulous historical scholarship sustained by a compelling commitment to decency, so effective precisely because it does not preach but lets the truth emerge from the facts and from responsible interpretations.

Drafted as a common soldier, Bracher served in the German army, was captured in North Africa, and spent some months in a prison camp in Kansas; this experience with American democracy, intensified by postwar studies at Harvard and coupled with his distaste for totalitarianism, determined the direction he would take as a historian. I found all this instructive enough, but his wife, Dorothee, proved an even more compelling source for me, through her family story rather than any explicit teaching. She was the daughter of Rüdiger Schleicher, whose wife was a Bonhoeffer. The Bonhoeffers, whether jurists or preachers, were unorthodox Christians who took their religion seriously. In their months of travail in prison, under torture, and facing the prospect of death, they regularly turned to passages from the Bible. Detesting Hitler and his gang on aesthetic, political, and simply human grounds, and seeing no end as long as he remained alive, they decided after long hesitation to participate in a scheme to assassinate him. The Führer's death became for them an article of faith.

That faith destroyed the circle. The attempt on Hitler's life on July 20, 1944, failed, and the conspirators were discovered. Schleicher, a conscientious public servant but a consistent anti-Nazi whose participation in the plot was marginal, was arrested, condemned to death, and, while the Russian troops were about to storm Berlin, shot on April 23, 1945. His brother-in-law, Klaus Bonhoeffer, was executed on the same day. Another brother-in-law, Hans von Dohnanyi, had shared the same fate on April 9, the day that the spiritual leader of the group, Dietrich Bonhoeffer, was also put to death.

In the course of our year at the Center, we had seen the Brachers socially and become good if not intimate friends. Until the day of their departure for home, we knew nothing of this history. For some reason, as we drove them to the airport, they began to talk, and I remember thinking—perhaps even saying—Why, you lost more members of your family to these barbarians than I did! This may sound like a peculiar response, as though the discovery of good Germans depended on some quantitative comparison, as though the fate of millions could be reduced to a body count. I do not want to defend it, I can only say that this is how I felt. I must have been ready to listen.

We did not venture into Germany for another three or four years, but after that we began to visit the country until it became something of a habit. We took an automobile tour through German museums, we stayed with the Brachers in Bonn, we did research in German archives. And we came to Berlin often, sometimes staying for months, with feelings strikingly different from the difficult first attempt in 1961. Eventually we came to feel more or less at home in the city of my birth, though I want to stress the "more or less." And we rediscovered Emil Busse in the late 1960s, when we were staying in Berlin and it suddenly occurred to me to look for him. Much had happened, well over a decade had passed since we had last heard from him, but why not try? There was one Emil Busse listed in the telephone book, and I wrote to him: "Are you the Emil Busse who . . . ?" The next day there came an excited telephone call: he was.

The next few days we did little but talk—or, better, listen. For Busse was, and is, a gripping narrator: precise, voluble, and credible. He told us about his adventures in the war, an anti-Nazi trying to preserve his political principles as much as his life. Determined not to be forced to shoot at Allied soldiers, whom after all he regarded as his friends and potential liberators from Nazi tyranny, he stayed out of the draft as long as he could by joining the police. But when the German armed forces, having suffered great losses in the East, cast about for more cannon fodder, he could no longer dodge forcible enlistment. It was then that he decided to mime a progressive disease; he would be suffering from crippling sciatica. But to do so convincingly he first had to study how sciatica hurts and where, for a physician examining someone who claims to have the ailment knows that it does not attack the whole body uniformly. So Busse went to school to a politically reliable friend who was actually subject to sciatica. The stage set, he then gradually acquired the symptoms, hurting, he told everyone, more and more. The army doctors, alert to malingerers trying to evade military service, probed him again and again, but Busse was convincing. He ate little if anything, he lost weight, he moved with the greatest difficulty, he even allowed himself to become incontinent in his hospital bed. Nothing helped, not even the most sophisticated medication. A grave case!

But sciatica, even at its most severe, also gradually comes to an end. The war lasted and lasted, and so, by late 1944, Busse found it politic to admit to a certain improvement. In early 1945, while the German armies were counterattacking in the Rhineland, he was declared well. Then a new summons came, and Busse performed his most heroic and most painful act: he poured boiling water over his thighs. When an army doctor screamed at him for his carelessness, he explained the accident as an innocent blunder: trying to heat up a bath for himself and still weak from his recent illness, he had slipped. We listened, we believed, we admired.

None of these tales, from Bracher to Busse, added up to my unconditional surrender. In Germany, conspicuously, almost truculently, I was an American; I found myself a vocal patriot, almost a chauvinist. Nothing incensed me more (as it still does) than Germans denigrating the United States as materialistic and uncultivated. Look who's talking! Nor did my new attitude mean that I took the Germans on trust. For me, they were on good behavior. During the academic year 1974–75 I was invited to stay in Munich as a guest of the university and, at the same time, to a one-year fellowship at

Wolfson College, Oxford. We decided that we would divide the year equally, staying first in Munich and afterward at Oxford. But Ruth and I also agreed that we would stay among Germans only as long as nothing got under our skin. At the first sign of anti-Semitism on their part, at the first sign of discomfort on ours, we would flee to Oxford. But the people we met or overheard on the bus, the stories we read in the newspapers gave us no cause for anti-German feelings, ready as we were for them. We stayed until January.

My scholarly interests, too, opened out. True, I had done my dissertation on a German, but that was safe enough; Eduard Bernstein was, as I have said, both a Jew and a Marxist. But in the two volumes on the Enlightenment which I published in 1966 and 1969, Kant, Lessing, and Wieland had their moments on the stage; and in my five-volume study on the Victorian bourgeoisie, published between 1984 and 1998, I paid as much attention to German psychologists, politicians, painters, novelists, and literary critics as I did to their British, French, or American counterparts.

I am listing these publications not to parade my writings but to indicate that I had, after a long struggle, managed to integrate Germany and Germans into the culture of modern Western civilization, which had become my favorite hunting ground. At the same time, I had integrated Germany into my self-perception—but by no means so completely. Even the work I did on German and Austrian culture showed traces of the old feelings, though not, I like to think, to its detriment as scholarship. In 1967 I was invited to write a long essay on Weimar culture to serve as an introduction to a bulky collective volume of essays on the impact of German refugees on the United States. I can still recall that I put everything else aside and wrote it quickly—it was published in 1968—with intense engagement.

My *Weimar Culture* turned out to be an elegy for a failed experiment. I can defend my reading of the republic's short history as accurate, even (I hope) insightful, but an unmistakable air of mourning hangs over it. My concluding paragraph is shadowed by suicides, of Max Liebermann's aged widow, of Walter Benjamin, of Stefan Zweig, of other talented writers. By January 30, 1933, I wrote, "Adolf Hitler was Chancellor of Germany, and the men of Weimar scattered, taking the spirit of Weimar with them, into the Aesopianism of internal migration, into death in the extermination camps, into suicide—suicide in a Berlin apartment after a knock on the door, on the Spanish frontier, in a rented flat in Paris, in a Swedish village, in a Brazilian town, in a New York hotel room. But others took the spirit of Weimar into life, into great careers and lasting influence in laboratories, in hospitals, in journalism, in theatres, in universities, and gave that spirit its true home, in exile." This is not the cool prose of a distant observer.

In the biography of Freud I published a decade later, in 1988, I found myself driven by the same reminiscent passion as I came to the last two years of his life. My family and I had learned in March 1938 from Radio Strasbourg that the Austrians had greeted Hitler and celebrated his invasion of their country with anti-Semitic vandalism, joyful pillage, and no less joyful murder. But I had never followed up these events until I did research on the life of Freud. I read newspapers, I read memoirs, I read historians, and it all was only too horribly familiar, that large-scale dress rehearsal for what I had seen on November 10, 1938, as I bicycled through the aftermath of Kristallnacht. I was not disposed to forgive those who did not deserve forgiveness.

Yet my shift was admittedly drastic, and remained, as I went through it, a purely private matter, shared with only a few of my closest friends. After all, strong feelings about Germans continued to run high in the United States decades after the collapse of the Nazi regime, and I did not expect that my inward journey would be generally appreciated. I was right. I must here insert an experience that I have already reported in the preface to *Freud, Jews, and Other Germans*, a collection of essays I published in 1978. Two years before, I had written a pair of op-ed pieces on "Thinking About the Germans" for the *New York Times*. I told, briefly, of the background I have canvassed at greater length in this memoir and concluded that, considering my friendships with Germans and the increasing number of Germans too young to have had anything to do with the Nazis, I no longer subscribed to the saying that the only good German is a dead German. The response was a wholly unanticipated flood of comments. Invitations to discuss my newfound objectivity abounded. More than seventy-five letters and postcards applauded or denounced my stand. Some malicious prankster subscribed to a number of magazines in my name, and I had to spend a good deal of time extricating myself from these involuntary obligations.

What was particularly remarkable was the variety of opinions. Those who had understood my message either praised me for being reasonable about the Germans (significantly, it was German refugees like me who fell into this category) or damned me for selling out. The others (and there were many) professed to admire me, or to despise me, for saying publicly that the only good German is a dead German. I learned something I should have known before: reading is largely a Rorschach test. It is disheartening but true: we get out of texts largely what we put into them.

I have sometimes been asked whether I have detected any continuity in my work, some thread linking up my first book, published in 1952, and my latest, published in early 1998. This question tends to be accompanied by the commonplace that authors write only one book. I confess that I do not recognize such single-mindedness in my work except that it is dominated by a lasting desire to find things out or set things straight. But that is necessary equipment for any serious historian and does not differentiate me from my colleagues. I have written on invitation when I thought I had something to say that had not been said, or on my own impulsion when I thought that the existing literature called out for revision. Because I never undertook revisions for their own sake, to set things right did not appear to me, as it did to Hamlet, a cursed spite. If anything, my commitment to a psychoanalytic approach, which permits the historian to dig more deeply than with other auxiliary disciplines, has only supported my abiding curiosity about the past. If some deem it necessary to connect my work to my six years under the Nazis, I should think my variety of interests rather than their uniformity would be pertinent. They show, at least to me, that over the years I have managed largely to free myself from the poisons in my past and go my own way.

There are refugees—we all know them—to whom their life under the Nazis, outwardly very similar to my own, has obsessed them without cease and without recourse. For them, wrestling with the Holocaust has become a vocation in itself. This is a familiar phenomenon even among professional historians who dig into the German past, sometimes as far back as Luther, to find premonitions of Nazism or fundamental causal conditions throughout the centuries that made Hitler predictable, almost inescapable. I understand this preoccupation but I do not share it. In my judgment it is in essence unhistorical. Yet none of this respect for complexity, I must insist, has compromised my willingness to recognize and condemn pure villainy when I see it.

But my concession to permit, even to encourage, the strongest possible denunciations of Nazis does not meet one objection to my professionalism that I must take seriously. If some refugees have been obsessed with the Holocaust, have I been obsessed with an effort to recoil from it? I do not think so, but I recognize that others might see me this way. It is notoriously true that we are poor judges of ourselves, and the person we glimpse in the mirror may bear imagined no less than real traits. The truth is, I must confess, that I have deliberately refused to dwell on the mass murder of Europe's

Jews. I have avoided movies that deal with it, even important ones, like *Shoah*. I have not yet been to the Holocaust Museum in Washington. When in the mid-1980s we had an opportunity to visit Auschwitz, my wife went alone. We all have our defenses to help us get through life, and these happen to be mine. I am not proud of them, but I see no need to apologize for them. Surely my record of hard work shows that I have not fled to hedonism to erase my past. Freud said that the most effective—or, rather, the least ineffective—way of dealing with misery is work, and I can testify that Freud was right.

What does all this tell us about Berlin and me? The truth is that after all this long recital I do not feel unambiguous enough to be as dogmatic as some readers might want me to be. I have, to use an all-too-popular expression, no closure to offer. When I was in Tel Aviv a dozen years ago and my non-Jewish Jewishness came under discussion at lunch, a shrewd Israeli novelist asked me whether I turn up the sound when, listening to the radio, I hear the newscaster pronounce the name Israel. It was a good question. If we apply it to the issue I have explored in this memoir, am I still a Berliner? In 1962, visiting my birthplace, President Kennedy made the wildly cheered immortal remark *Ich bin ein Berliner*. The phrase has received a good deal of pedantic criticism, since *Ich bin Berliner* might have been more idiomatic, and his dictum could be read to mean that he had declared himself to be a jelly doughnut. I find this cavil ridiculous, but in any event what matters is what I can legitimately say about myself. I *am* a Berliner, or I *was* a Berliner?

Speaking as tentatively as I must, I would say that I am no longer a Berliner in the way I was before 1933 and never will be again. This does not mean that the name Berlin does not evoke something special in me. I still root for Hertha B.S.C. I still regret architectural adventurism that is working toward effacing the unique atmosphere of the city. I still bristle when the city is being maligned, as I did recently upon reading a sour and, I thought, ill-informed article about Berlin in the *New York Review of Books*. When it comes to Berlin, I am something of a conservative; walking around the Potsdamer Platz, where capitalist giants like Mercedes Benz and Sony are erecting massive advertisements for themselves which war with Berlin's horizontality, I feel I have glimpsed the reshaping of its identity, and it rather worries me. And I would profoundly regret it if I could not see my Berlin friends again; I have always treasured friendship, and at least one of my Berlin intimates is as close to me as any I have been fortunate to acquire in America.

Today, as I write these words, is August 27, 1997. In this morning's *New York Times* there is an article about a highly regarded and most influential German political pollster, Elisabeth Noëlle-Neumann. Her association with Goebbels's propaganda ministry between 1940 and 1942 has been known for several years, but now an American academic, Christopher Simpson, has charged that she not only played ball with the regime but shaded her researches and falsified her results to serve the Third Reich. Dr. Noëlle-Neumann has vehemently denied this allegation and suggested that in fact she had worked for the government because she "opposed the Nazis by working from within." Her insulting remarks about Jews dating from the war years—according to her, Jews totally controlled and thus destroyed the reliability of the American press—had been written, she now claims, "under orders." To compound the confusion, the committee at American University considering tenure for Dr. Simpson received a number of "identical nasty" letters denigrating the candidate for daring to attack this giant of public opinion research. Did Noëlle-Neumann encourage or inspire these letters, or were they sent without her knowledge or approval?

My own information about the case is limited to the newspaper story, but I have already made up my mind. Noëlle-Neumann is guilty until she is proved innocent. Is that fair? Is that objective? Is that scientific? Certainly not. It only shows that Peter Fröhlich of 1938 and 1939 is still alive in Peter Gay in 1997. Will I change my mind? Perhaps. Who knows? After all, my scholarly life is not yet over. And whatever projects pique my curiosity in the future, a trace of Berlin—the city, the memory, the cherished and hated object of my ambivalence—is likely to figure in it somehow. We historians know that it is perilous to make predictions about things to come; it is almost as perilous to make predictions about historical works to come. So much depends on historians' becoming interested in, indeed impassioned about, a class, a battle, a personage, an idea previously scorned, neglected, or misunderstood. After all, historians, despite the well-known limitations that fallible human nature imposes upon them, are, to use an unfashionable phrase, committed to the pursuit of truth, to an understanding of the realities the past has left behind. And so I must conclude without a forecast. As the Germans say at the end of an installment of a novel serialized in a newspaper, *Fortsetzung folgt*. To be continued.

Acknowledgments

My principal debt is to Gladys Topkis, who succeeded in breaking the logjam of my hesitations and loos-
ening my inhibitions over my private history. I have always
enjoyed writing. But recounting my German travail, this exploration of my world and myself during a stretch of six years
that it would be tame to call "unpleasant," proved the least
exhilarating assignment I have ever given myself or received
from others. Hence Gladys's mixture of firmness and kindness was decisive for me, and I am deeply grateful to her.
She not only pressed me to write this book but then edited
it with her customary mastery of the small as much as the
large issues.

Gladys was in good company. Other friends also propelled
me in the right direction: Henry and Jane Turner, Al and
Ruth Burstein, Bill and Shirley Kahn. In Berlin, I greatly
benefited from conversations with Gaby Katwan as informative as they were affectionate; her keen sense of the tension
between fantasy and reality, and her brilliant suggestions,
smoothed my way. Klaus Schulz did some impressive research to shore up my selective memory and reduce my
equally selective amnesia. Doron Ben-Atar cheered me along
the way. It was good to have Dan Heaton go over my man-

uscript, for he fully understands my love of soccer and my passion for Arsenal.

Several of my relatives, notably my cousin Jack Gay, unstintingly answered my sometimes inconvenient questions. I want also to thank Paul Kwilecki for a lively correspondence, and Comer Gay (Edgar's widow) and Christine Kohnke, for finding and transmitting some valuable documents.

My debt, and my parents' debt, to Emil Busse is only too obvious. His willingness to remember—precisely, colorfully, reliably—was as essential to my book as his help in the desperate days of 1938–39 was essential, in even more consequential ways, to our survival. As always, my wife, Ruth, an uncertified but authentic historian of modern Jewry, read every version of the manuscript and greatly contributed to my self-understanding as we unceasingly discussed my all-consuming topic.